How to Go On After the Loss of Your Mother

A Life-Changing Guide to Stop Feeling Guilty, Forgiving Yourself, and Coping with Grief and Loss

Melanie Aniston

1

Table of Contents

Introduction

L osing your mother is a life-changing episode; you can never prepare enough for when the time comes. This is the furthest thought from anyone's mind; and when it happens, it feels unreal and hard to believe. How can someone who has raised and given you so much love, no longer be around? How will life go on? If your mother was severely ill before passing, perhaps you saw it coming, but it does not mean that you can accept it. When the news hits you, it feels like breathing is a difficult task, your chest hurts, and you freeze.

This is something no one teaches us to deal with - not at school and not in life. You do not know what to do and neither do those around you, from your closest friends to your colleagues. If you are in a relationship, your partner knows this is a difficult time for you, but they do not necessarily know how to comfort you and deal with the situation. You need support and massive care. If you have recently lost your mother, she passed years ago but you still struggle, or a close friend or family member recently lost their mother, then this book is for you.

Dealing with such a sad situation can feel isolating and hard; although you want to seek help and adapt to the new norm, you do not know where to start. People talk about it, often years down the line; but when it happens, you may find it hard to find helpful sources at first, especially without guidance. Death may be a taboo subject in certain cultures and not be talked about much. Your mother is your role model, guardian, and the main carer of the home.

During the best times spent together, you imagined she would live forever, or at least you hoped so. Right after the loss, you think life is so unfair and wonder why SHE had to go. If you are not surrounded by those who have experienced the same struggle, you might find it difficult to find someone who can understand. Everyone knows that death is part of our lifecycle, but it feels remote until it hits.

Losing a mom may bring on dark times and leave you devastated physically and mentally, but there are ways to overcome it by creating and maintaining a support circle around you. You can learn how to practice self-care, seek help, and finally adapt. Everyone deals with the loss of their mother differently, and no grief is the same. Knowledge and awareness, however, are important at this difficult time. Your heart needs to heal, and this takes time and knowledge. You must allow yourself to feel the way you do.

Life must go on. Those around you might also need to adapt to help you. If you have a circle of close friends you trust and feel comfortable with, tell them about the loss so they can become your support system. Do not feel obligated to socialize or meet with them during this time, but there are ways of slowly getting back to your usual routine after a loss, with slight adaptations.

If you have siblings also grieving the loss of your mother, you will want to support each other and try your best to avoid family feuds. A funeral can be hard to get through from planning to attending it. If you have a large family, that can be another challenge. If you have never experienced the loss of a relative, this can be difficult and new at the same time.

Asking for help to organize the funeral and how to take care of your mother's possessions will be the last thing on your mind. Besides, it is very challenging to ask a close friend about these processes if you know they have lost a parent before. You would be revisiting a dark episode in their life, one they would not feel very comfortable talking about.

Support will help you deal with the turmoil of emotions you are currently experiencing. This should help you and your family members build a stronger bond rather than arguing about trivial things or material belongings. Your father might need you to keep things afloat because he too is struggling with the loss.

The loss of a loved one can lead to depression, anxiety, a lack of performance at work, failed relationships, and a lack of self-care. Learn to identify normal grief and when it leans towards depression and needs professional assistance. Although this is not easy, you can do it! Learn how to be around things that remind you of her and how to get by on those special occasions that remind you of your mother like Mother's Day, her birthday, and the holiday season. Learn how to find happiness again, adapt to going on in life without her, accepting reality, and seek help when you need. You must understand how such a loss affects you physically and mentally. If you have a close friend who recently lost their own mother, know what not to say and how to support and comfort them. Grief is not an external life event, but it affects both the body and mind. If you are a man and feel your reaction is different than your sister's - or your wife who lost hers a couple of years back - understand that grief affects men and women differently.

You are your mother's legacy, and her memory will live in you. You may not be able move on after her life has ended, but it does not mean that yours is over. This loss will change the way you look at life and others around you. Make sure this makes you a stronger individual with the values your mother taught. You are who you are because of her, and no one can take that away from you.

Learn how to rekindle the joy you have for the things you enjoy the most, without feeling guilty that you are allowing yourself to be happy after the loss. Know that you are carrying your mom's memory with you wherever you go, and the one thing she wanted you to be - whether she is are around or not - is to be happy! It's possible that saying it is easier than doing it, but there are ways to cope and accept that life will now take a different form. Although looking back jogs your memory to the happiest moments of your life, you must not get stuck in the past as it will hinder your progress.

Make it clear that you need space and wanting to be alone is normal at this dire time. Right after the death of your mother, you might feel angry, especially if you did not have enough time to say goodbye or struggled seeing her suffer (if terminally ill). You might think life is unfair and ask why this had to happen to you. The thing is, everyone feels their loss is the hardest, and it probably is for them.

But everyone is carrying their weight, so do not compare the death of someone else to your mother's. Grief with all its different stages will be explained, but that does not mean you must go through these stages exactly as described. You must know what is going on in your brain and how it impacts you physically, but grief is not a linear process and varies from individual to individual.

You cannot get over a death completely, but you can learn to deal and live with it, without letting it impact your life negatively, even years after it happens. Accept that things, places, and most days are going to remind you of her, and that is just fine. You will eventually see these triggers as memories. You can learn to live through your daily routine without succumbing to depression or anxiety.

You might want to devote yourself to a new hobby, work longer hours, or go out with your friends more as a healthy distraction. You will eventually come around to celebrate Mom rather than mourn her. What you are about to read should help you find comfort and teach you to overcome the hurdles. There is enough knowledge and awareness here to help you acknowledge and identify the challenges.

If a friend recently lost their mother to cancer or she passed away naturally, know that you can support them even with little things. Show them that you are there to listen. Deal with the awkward silence by showing you are there if they need to talk. If someone at the office recently lost their mother, know what to send and how to treat them upon their return. If you come from different cultures, the way they celebrate death may be different than what you do, so learn how to adopt an open mind and set any cultural differences aside.

Support may be required more than just a few weeks after the loss, so you need to know when to be there. Learn what to say and understand that the last thing they want to hear about are your trivial problems, like the minor hiccups in your dating life. They should be gaining something from their perspective. You must learn not to take things too personally and understand that what they might say or how they treat you right now is not a true representation of what they think about you.

Their behavior is governed by this life-changing event. Although they might not show it, they are thankful for your presence when they need to talk and appreciate that you how to act around them right now. You may feel like nothing you say or do can help, but that is not the case.

Adapting the right approach after the loss can help you create a safe space to move forward; even after she is gone, you can have a normal life, experience emotions, enjoy others, while carrying her memory with you.

Chapter 1:

The Loss

I f you have recently lost your mother, whether it has been months or years, you probably still remember the day you found out. Your mind might want to block the negative event, but you somehow always remember this moment vividly. Your brain may filter things you want to remember but block others you wish to forget. You most likely have one memory that sticks out the most, like having to tell your younger siblings of the loss or remembering the last goodbyes. These memories may be the ones that come to mind the last thing before you go to sleep at night.

Of course, memories and flashbacks differ. A flashback is slightly more intense than a memory and feels like it is taking over your body entirely. You feel like you are experiencing the event again. Flashbacks bring sudden and uncontrollable negative feelings, more associated with nightmares. A flashback is more like a sensory experience while memory is a thought process usually acquired to refer to later. After the loss of your mother, you probably have plenty of memories and tend to hold on to the most positive ones. You can recall your late mother and go over the memories with close friends or relatives to honor her presence. You may still experience bad memories, but a bad memory has less impact on your body than a flashback.

The night following the loss may be a sleepless one, and you may not have managed to close an eye. That is normal. The following days may be governed by a lack of self-care, malnutrition, and loads of crying. Having someone around who has experienced this even years ago should comfort you. Siblings or close relatives may assist you with the daily chores in the days following the loss.

To the other extreme, days after the loss, you may feel like not getting out of bed; and if you did, it would be because you had to see to your younger siblings and not because you voluntarily wanted to. Soon after losing your mother, you may find yourself in the darkest of places, and that is perfectly normal. Know you will not be there forever. It does take time to see the light again and feel happy at times. You will feel like you are in a dark place sometimes. There are no clear instructions for when to feel sad or happy.

Grieving loved ones is different for everyone, and you should not feel ashamed if a happy memory of your late mother comes to mind and brings the slightest smile to your face. Healing brings happy moments more frequently, but this does not take away from your dark moments. People who have lost their mothers confirm that although they may never feel like their life goes back to full normality because a huge part is missing, normality is achievable after a full year has passed after the loss.

One needs to go through her birthday, the next holiday season, and Mother's Day and adapt. When years pass, one recalls getting over these occasions and how to deal with those emotions that take over during these days. The first year can prove to be a challenge, but it does get better.

If you have recently lost your mother, you may experience waves of sadness. The more recent the loss, the more frequent these episodes will be. Initially, you may experience them every few hours, but they should lessen in frequency as time goes by. At first, you may look at the simplest of things or listen to a song and instantaneously you are taken the memory of your late mother. These episodes may never go away; but eventually, with the right support system and self-care, you will learn to deal with them, get them less often, and look at them as distant, positive memories. When the frequency of these waves lessens, it means you are moving forward, although it might not feel as such.

If you are reading this and wonder whether you will ever fully heal, know that it takes time. The goal is not to cancel this tragic event from your memory but learn to deal with it by filtering only the positive impact your mother had made on you. If you have experienced the loss recently, healing can seem faraway for now. If your mother died years ago, you may feel like you are almost fully healed but not completely.

Healing does not mean that you no longer miss your mother. It may feel hard to understand the concept of getting better at this time but know that it does. Besides the many things others can do to help you get there, there are plenty of things you can do for yourself to get better. Right after the loss, many people will tell you that it will get better; and although you wouldn't be feeling that way, trust the process. You may strongly believe this pain will never get better, and this negative notion is perfectly normal. A day will come when you look back and realize that it did get better. You can finally get out of bed, socialize, and enjoy life again.

A part of your mother lives in you; and by enjoying your life and moving forward, you are honoring her presence, not disrespecting her. Right now, you may feel overwhelmed with guilt and look back at so many things you could have done to change the order of things; but know that you will start laughing more and engage in social activities. The impact your mother left on you and the way she shaped you can never be taken away.

Her death may change your perspective on life and the way you deal with things in general afterward. You may think of her every day, whether she passed recently or years ago. When someone dies, you suffer several losses. Recognizing what you have lost is a big part of grieving, and loss brings a lot of changes that are not always obvious. There is the loss of the person's physical presence, as well as other less tangible losses, including the thoughts you shared, your social life, and all the nice things the deceased did for you.

You may find yourself talking to your late mom and reminiscing. You may recall moments when she was sick (if she passed because of an illness) or times when she helped you finish a project or stayed up with you all night after your first break up.

You are not required to move on, just move forward with your life while carrying your mother with you. Keep caring for her legacy and make her proud of what you have become because of her. Although she is not physically with you, she is still a part of you. Embrace the bond you had with your mother.

Chapter 2:
Resolving Family Conflict After the Loss

F amilies are brought to their knees by death, bringing out their best and worst. It can feel like a second loss when friends and families fight after a death. You are coping with the death of a loved one and then your support system becomes unsupportive and a source of emotional pressure. Please know that you are not alone if this has happened to you. Many people can relate to family turmoil following a death. What is the most prevalent reason for the problem? Fighting over materialistic things: you have predicted it.

As difficult as it is for many of us to concede, countless families who never imagined they would disagree over material possessions are suddenly engulfed by disputes over plots of land and assorted possessions.

Death's Aftermath

Be prepared to experience changed dynamics after the loss of the mother in a family. Your late mother might have kept the family together so that members may drift apart following her loss. This happens for many reasons. Some families may have maintained a bond solely for the sake of the late mother. If siblings grow apart after her death, it could be because the other person reminds them of the deceased or if relatives show a different side of themselves.

After or before the mother was ill, familiar member may change their perceptions and opt to grow apart. If the mother was the one who organized the family events and has now passed, there may no longer be an interest in socializing and reuniting if someone is blamed for the loss; it may push the person away from the rest of their family, whether their assumptions are genuine or not. Some family members may avoid talking about the loss and expect others do the same. To prevent such occasions; they avoid getting together.

It is imperative to avoid conflict as it might be hard to make up. Rivalry can turn adults into children that refuse to reason things out. If you feel like your siblings are not being honest after your mother's death, do not assume that acting the same way will solve the issues. Be the one who breaks the pattern. Be honest about the will, your feelings, and the way you feel things should be dealt with. You may get to a point where you are no longer able to bear the sight of certain family members, but this is not always the case for everyone. It can be difficult to cope with the loss of a loved one while being surrounded by family.

Although you usually look forward to spending time with family members, your behavior is perfectly acceptable during this time. All you can do, despite your best efforts, is set a good example for others to follow. It is important to remember that you might not be able to change their minds to keep your peace of mind.

If your siblings are constantly quarrelings and causing family discord, know that they are unlikely to change their ways, especially if it has been going on for decades. Just make it a point to set the right tone and avoid leaving room for conflict to arise. Kindness, respect, and a listening ear are all things you can offer. It is entirely up to your family members to decide what to do next. Be a good role model and, hopefully, your family will recognize that remaining calm will aid them in navigating the situations.

In general, avoid having a conversation with someone who is yelling and shouting. If they are in your face, it may be difficult to remain calm, but try to do so if possible. Demonstrate empathy and understanding to family members. Give a little more to those prone to misbehaving, as they require graciousness and kindness more than ever. Kindness is a strength, not a flaw. While you wish you could scream at your obnoxious brother, choose kindness instead. Finally, you want everyone to live in harmony. Your generosity can serve as an example. Hopefully, someone else in your family shares your sentiments. Others will notice your kindness the more you show it.

If the conflict between family members cannot be managed, do not be afraid to seek help from professional mediators. These trained individuals can help you and your family get through the basic logistics of the funeral ceremony, sorting out belongings, the will, and other assets. Allow them to handle the heavy lifting. A neutral third party can keep things from becoming too emotional. High levels of conflict can be draining, and a mediator is trained to help things run better. You, as a family member, can focus on the above helpful hints with less effort if a professional is in charge.

If you are worried about conflict, you might want to talk to the mediator ahead of time. They not only offer additional advice, but you can also call on them for assistance if things get out of hand. Some family members may object to the involvement of a third party. Assure them that a neutral third party can assist everyone in working together more effectively. After some time following the loss and once the will and belongings are sorted out, you may consider individual or family counseling to help rekindle the damaged relationship with your siblings from material feuds. Keep in mind that you cannot change a greedy person's heart. You can, however, be kind while maintaining mental stability.

Sorting through possessions

A common conflict after the loss can be when to sort through the mother's possessions. Some may feel like they are ready to do so right after her death, while others may require more time. If there is no will in place, it may be a bigger struggle to determine who gets what. Even if there a will in in place, it may not cover household or other sentimental things, leaving room for conflict. It is normal to feel emotionally attached to material things, especially if something reminds you of your mother.

Some family members may feel like you are fixating on trivial things when you contemplate keeping that pocket mirror your mother used to carry with her everywhere she went. Some may be quick to discard such items, while others may feel that these things will remind them of their mother.

Your mother's house carries a lot of sentimental value to family members, making them want to retain her house rather than sell it. Every room can remind you of your mother and selling the house may mean you have to go over her belongings, further saddening you if you have yet to move on. Others may disagree and would rather sell it to get the financial return in hand. A common familial conflict after the mother's death is over money.

Siblings may gather money collectively to pay for the funeral, so money comes into play here. After a loss, not having a will in place can exacerbate the financial situation. The family member must come to terms with the conclusion of their physical relationship with the deceased person as well as their continued grief. Unfortunately, at a time when the family might profit from getting together more than ever, misunderstandings and disagreements sometimes keep them apart.

Many relatives become puzzled as they find themselves at war over a loved one's material belongings. They do not usually show their love in the form of presents, items, or money as a family. Their beliefs have never been based on materialism. Yet again, they find themselves arguing over material things their late mother left behind. This does not mean that some family members are not truly greedy and opportunistic; but in most cases, family members are grieving, and their behavior is purely affected by the loss.

Grief makes us all a bit egoistic, making it impossible to see another person's feelings, acts, and grief responses from a different viewpoint. Anxiety and confusion, two normal grief reactions, will raise a person's propensity to believe that others see it in the same as they do. Human brains are prone to making assumptions about people they are close to and like them, such as family members because they assume they share values, attitudes, and worldview.

People tend to assign other people's actions to personal characteristics such as envy and selfishness rather than considering psychological, emotional, or situational effects on behavior. If you are dealing with troublesome family members, the loss of a loved one can feel even more daunting; but there are ways to reduce conflict and take care of yourself as you go through this difficult time. It can be difficult to avoid getting sucked into family turmoil, especially when some members appear to be greedy.

Allow others to express how they feel about sorting through their mother's belongings; and if they need more time, reach a compromise. If you are the one experiencing these feelings, though, you may feel more detached and disconnected from your kin. People will have empathy and understanding with one another in an ideal universe, but it is sometimes easier said than done.

If someone feels like being in control helps them get over the loss, it can be helpful for other family members to pitch in and guide that energy toward the right thing like planning the funeral ceremonies and clearing out the clutter in the house. When one family member is ready to pack, sell, or get rid of the deceased person's possessions while another is not, there will be general confusion. The family member not ready may perceive the other as pushy, callous, uncaring, selfish, or eager to move on too soon.

One family member may be eager to go through a deceased relative's possessions, while another cannot bear the idea. Neither is correct nor incorrect; they are simply grieving at varying rates. Some people grieve by acting by taking care of their loved one's possessions. Someone who avoids dealing with such possessions perceives them as grief triggers, hence their avoidance.

Your family member may be reaching for things that once belonged to your loved one because those items have come to mean a lot and have more sentimental than a monetary value. Holding on to physical items can also be an escape, whereby relatives stash material things of their late mother in the hope that their bond remains longer. This is done mostly when acceptance has not yet taken place, and one strives to keep physical closeness to the person they lost. If you've ever behaved impulsively during an emotional episode by saying or doing something you came to regret, you should trust that now is not the time to throw away souvenirs, knickknacks, photographs, and other reminders of your loved one, especially if they bring up sadness and tears while your grief is still raw.

These irreplaceable tangible connections between you and someone you love could be lost forever once they are hauled to the curb and removed. As a result, as you grieve, you should put off throwing out any items connected to your loved one. You may feel differently after some time, perhaps six months or a year, as you adjust to life after the death of a loved one. At the very least with the passage of time, you will be better equipped to assess what you truly want to keep and what you want to toss.

Ideally, big decisions like selling your mom's house are left for later when you are in a better position to make such an important decision. Unfortunately, this may not always be possible; there are wills and other siblings to deal with. Belongings like a house need to be cleared and put up for sale very soon after the death. Financial issues are the most common problems that people feel compelled to address right away. If your loved one left you with a mountain of bills and insurance paperwork, enlist the help of a friend who is a bookkeeper, accountant, or otherwise well-suited to such tasks.

Though some items may have deadlines and consequences if not handled immediately, it is just as important to prioritize to keep your sanity. This differs from one person to the next. If they cannot bag everything up and start getting rid of it right away, some people feel like they are losing their minds. Others choose to keep everything in its original location for as long as possible.

There is no one-size-fits-all approach to grieving, as with so many other things in life. Planning, on the other hand, is almost always beneficial. Putting everything in a bag and throwing it away without thinking is not a good idea. It is also not a good idea to put off going through items for years because you do not want to deal with it. Putting things that mean so much to you away can be very difficult, so if a friend can help, list what you wish to have around. If you are putting it off, set a goal with to get started. Make sure to ask ahead of time and be as specific as possible.

Throwing or giving away items that are valuable to other family members can lead to arguments. One item that has no sentimental value to one family member may have significant sentimental value to another. Do not assume you know what is important to other family members. Try to define how you are going to about around clearing things. This could be determined by priority and can be a difficult process. Keep in mind that you are likely to come across items you have not seen in a long time, as constant reminders of the person you have lost. It is tempting to want to do everything at once, but taking breaks is necessary if things become too overwhelming.

Once you started sorting things out, think of what you want to keep, what you wish to donate, what has a potential to be re-sold, and what needs to be thrown away. You may keep a box for things you are not sure what to do with to revisit later. Try not to overdo this and whenever possible, sort things out straight away instead of putting them off. If your mother collected certain items, try not to keep duplicates; and before committing to keeping stuff, make sure you have space to store them.

Keep in mind that most things can be a memory are less likely to be of use. If possible, opt for photographing things before discarding them. Create a photobook of memories. This may be hard to do, especially in the beginning. Try creating a display of things you wish to keep as a memory so you can see them less as clutter and more of meaningful items.

If your mother loved collecting and reading books, create a corner where these books can be kept in the form of a library. They will not be in the way, but you would have not discarded something your mom loved so much. These can be a nice memory for you and may get you to take after your mother and enjoy reading again. If you feel like things your mother owned are better donated or re-sold, identify these items and call charities that will make great use of them. Organize a garage sale with the things you feel have potential to be re-sold.

This can be overwhelming to say the least so prepare to take a break. Place items in a save box and sort them later. Our best advice is to keep a positive attitude and surround yourself with people who love and support you. Though this can be a difficult task, it can also be therapeutic. You may experience sadness and burst into tears during the sorting process, but you can also share memories and laughter with your siblings.

The house

Selling a family home is a difficult decision no matter one's age, and it is made even more difficult when it is prompted by the loss of a parent. If there are no clear instructions, you and your siblings can discuss choices with a solicitor. Much of the decision-making will be influenced by how close someone is to the house. They may ask for a larger portion of the profit if they are assigned to deal with the sale given their advantageous geographical position. If this is the case, make sure the rest of the family agrees to it.

Do not jump into selling the house because your brothers or sisters may not be ready to sell right away. You should begin the cleaning and inspection process before putting it on the market, so be strategic while being receptive. Allow no big improvements such as painting without everyone's permission and knowledge. Conversely, if you are having trouble coming to terms with the possibility of losing the family house, speak up. Your siblings will most likely understand that you need time to adapt to so many big changes and they might even be glad that you spoke up first because they may be feeling the same way but held back their reservations.

If they are not understanding, just ask them to value your sentiments and wait at least a month before deciding to sell. Explain that this is a significant tragedy for you and dealing with it all at once is too difficult in the aftermath of your mother's death. Throughout the process of burying a parent, compassion and integrity will be your most valued assets, particularly when it comes to your siblings.

Treatment for the terminally ill

Conflict can also start before the mother dies, especially if she was terminally ill and the siblings could not agree on treatment and end of life decisions. Even if not terminally ill, siblings could have disagreed on care options and hospitals. Some may have divided the responsibility of taking care of Mom to always be available for her, while other family members might struggle to care for her and end up outsourcing caregiving duties.

Arrangements after death also leave room for conflict, like cremation, funeral service, and burial location. The bigger the family, the more opinions, so conflict can be higher. The death of a mother can cause families to relocate. If your mother used to look after the kids while you were away, for example, and has now passed, you might want to move closer to your mother-in-law so she may take over that same duty since geographically it is more convenient for you to move now.

Moving may mean you spend less time traveling back and forth to pick up your kids, and you are located closer to someone who can give you a hand. If, after the death of a mother, children become orphans and custody rights must be handed over, conflict may arise until it is decided who will be the new carer of these children.

Family members grieving differently

Another top reason for conflict is that the grieving process is experienced differently. If your siblings think you are not very affected by the loss of your mother, they may feel you are moving on too quickly, or you may feel this way about them. But know that grieving is experienced and exhibited in various ways. It can be hard to tell when someone seems greedy because of grief or when they are truly greedy.

This can happen when a family unit, for example, is already malfunctioning before the death, and dynamics are worsened in this instance. Some may become insensitive to material possessions and their sentimental value after the loss. The financial needs of some siblings can influence their reactions when distributing the possessions of the deceased. If struggling financially, they may see the loss as an opportunity to regain financial stability, while others overtaken by grief and care find it less about financial gain and perceive the other's behavior as greedy. If you were the favored child, your sibling might unconsciously try to block you from receiving items because of their unprocessed parent-child emotions.

Develop empathy and try to comprehend their motivation. People who act out usually do so because they are in pain, which they may or may not be aware of. Siblings have an annoying tendency to irritate one another. If they try to provoke an argument, stay calm, be thoughtful, and know when to step away. Do not add to your already high level of stress. You may have thought this could never happen to your family because you are so close; grief and the stress it brings can turn things around.

You and your family may also struggle to reach a compromise on what is kept and what is given away or donated. Remember that the sentimental value you have with things is different from that of your siblings. Some may have it with material possessions, while others seek financial gain. Some families may disagree on whether to sell or keep the house because of the sentimental value versus the financial one.

Many people felt alone and misunderstood after a death. Family members are expected to look out for one another. For many people, the family has always been the anchor that holds them stable and the lighthouse that guides them through the storm. Grieving family members become uninterested and unable to act in the same manner as before.

People do not only contend with their loss but also with the fact that an important member of the family has passed away. Family members will have to fill some of the roles the loved one used to play; and when everyone changes, a drastic change in the way things have always been can occur. I believe we should all accept that our family status influences who we are as individuals, how we interact within the family unit, and the aspirations we have toward other family members. It is possible that the eldest child feels obligated to step in and provide for the mourning parent and younger siblings after a death. Perhaps the eldest child is obligated to take over many of their former responsibilities. Perhaps the youngest kid has been babied and now needs more emotional support.

Regardless, certain family members may feel abandoned or compelled to step into shoes they do not want to wear. In larger families, the whole dynamic becomes a bit more complex. However, where there is a significant age difference between the oldest and youngest children, it is worth considering that the family in which the oldest child grew up is very different from the family the youngest child experienced. This may reflect certain post-death variations in relationships and perspectives.

This can also be affected by cultures where by default, the oldest girl in the family takes over the motherly role when the mother passes away. It is the same when the father passes away, and the older boy needs to be the breadwinner. Death and mourning can cause people to behave irrationally, and it can severely disrupt a family's equilibrium. When a loss occurs within the family, there is a high risk of miscommunication as family members attempt to cope with shifting responsibilities and dynamics, diverse grieving types, and complex emotions.

Some people have the luck to find out that their family is exactly as loving and compassionate as they had hoped, but it is more normal to look to their family and feel saddened and uncertain. There is no definitive solution for family feuds after a loss, but you may take the coming suggestions to understand why conflict happens and how to deal with it.

People's brains work differently under stress. Some parts think reasonably, and some act on impulse and based on emotions. During stressful situations, the part that functions impulsively takes over, and it can be hard to use the rational side during these times. These parts are the prefrontal cortex, the area that struggles with reasoning, storing memories, and thinking in long term. If a lot of family members have recently lost someone dear to them, their brains are most likely reasoning using the prefrontal cortex. Therefore, conflict results from irrational decisions governed by emotions and stress.

Families are communities of individuals that are usually biologically related and reliant on one another. Each member has a distinct role to play and is required to react in accordance it. Maintaining the same pattern of behavior within a system can lead to both equilibrium and dysfunction. If a spouse is depressed and unable to get himself together, the wife may need to take on additional tasks to make up for it. The shift in roles may keep the relationship stable, but it may also drive the family toward a different baseline. The woman may not be able to continue her overachieving position, creating a new balance that may lead to instability. When a mother dies, the whole model is thrown off. Note that this does not happen if someone else from the family passes, but a mother has a very important role in the family, mostly holding things together, taking care of the house, and looking after the children.

Right after the death of a loved one, people often experience a lack of control, primarily because they are lost and feel they have no control over life such as who stays, and who goes. Some family members may want to regain control and plan the funeral ceremonies without asking for input from other family members. They may feel the need to sort through the late mother's belongings straight away while their siblings wish to take more time.

Grief can make you feel as if you are losing your mind. Your reaction to mourning, as well as the spectrum of emotions you have concerning the loss, will be unique to you. Some emotions associated with grief are despair, shock, sadness, isolation, guilt, and regret. It can be difficult to communicate with and encourage one another while each person is going through their own emotional experience. When someone you care about becomes suddenly furious, sad, nervous, or numb, your first instinct might be to wish they distance themselves from you.

Some grieve differently than others and attempt to take control over how relatives grieve the loss of their mother. Your spouse may be packing away the deceased mother's possessions before you realize it. They may be unable to speak about their deceased mother in an effort to escape the memories. When people are grieving, avoidance is frequently misinterpreted as a lack of care when, in fact, it is the result of extreme care.

The most common form of negative coping is avoidance. Negative coping includes activities such as drug abuse, keeping busy, and loneliness, as well as everything else you can do to numb, ignore, and reduce your reaction to grieving stimuli. Sometimes one or some family members take control because some others are struggling to even get out of bed due to grief and stress. Ideally, the person in control leaves room for others to voice their opinions.

Communication

A lack of communication can cause conflict, especially if some people are left out of an important decision they wish to be involved in. Try planning for how things can be handled and when. Get all the siblings together to go over the will and agree on who will be responsible for what. When the will is read to the entire family, those who feel left out or feel like assets were not distributed fairly may be left with a sense of bitterness, confusion, and questioning their entire past relationship with their late mother.

The person who can best explain the decisions taken on the will is no longer there to explain, and family members are left questioning. Create communication channels for everyone to be updated in real time. Always stay calm and avoid calling others names; if someone starts shouting, allow them to take a break, as decisions can only be made when everyone is calm. If someone is assigned to resell the house, communicate in family electronic chats to update everyone. If you had discussions with your late mother about her wishes following death, share these ideas with the rest of the family and avoid bringing non-immediate family members in.

More people means more opinions and more room for conflict. If cremation is an option, gather the views of the other family members and keep an open mind. Before you finalize the specifics, make sure that each sibling's questions and opinions have been discussed and respected. Do not reiterate the point; just let everybody know that you want to make sure no one is disappointed in the future. It's a deeply personal choice, and not everyone wants to share their thoughts. If any problems emerge, listen to your siblings and do your best to comprehend. Take the night off if possible and think about it to see where everything stands in the morning.

Make every attempt to ensure that everybody has an opportunity to talk, and no one is traumatized by the funeral as well as the loss. Another way to enhance communication and avoid conflict is to avoid accusing others and making statements that are expressive of your personal experience. Ideally, you will address the situation based on how you are feeling. Instead of accusing a relative of being insensitive for throwing your mother's clothes out, try explaining how you felt about what they did. If you accuse someone, they may get defensive because it is human nature. Focusing on your feelings instead leaves room for dialogue and discussions.

If you successfully manage to start a discussion, be open to their opinions as well because they probably have a valid reason for the way they acted. Grief can cause people to act insanely and regret what they have done soon after. If you recently lost your mother and your siblings do not seem like their usual selves, try to cut them some slack. Justify their behavior as a decision taken during an extraordinary life event and understand that they have made some poor choices.

The one poor choice they made does not override all the amazing memories you lived together and the respect you have shown to your late mother. Understand that these poor decisions were governed by emotions and impulsivity and are an exception to their character. You must be forgiving and understanding to yourself and the others around you living this same nightmare.

Tips for resolving family conflict

You can navigate using a few simple tips. Try setting the tone for how communication takes place because, ultimately, you cannot control how others talk to you. Try to focus on a uniting language and gather everyone in your statements, so all feel included. Listen actively because if someone is ignored, they are likely to get defensive and agitated. If you are overwhelmed or irritated by what someone has just said, step out of the conversation if you know you might lose it and escalate the situation.

Take a break and pause the conversation before it turns into an argument. Get back to it when you are calm and have thought things through. Before labeling some of your family members as greedy, try to empathize with them and understand that their behavior is governed by an overload of emotions and grief.

Make it a point to practice self-care during this time with meditation, grief journaling, seeking professional help from a grief therapist, enjoying time with pets if you have any, and read self-help literature on how to deal with grief. Make sure you let your siblings know when they exceed boundaries. Make it clear what you mean by space and when it is not acceptable for it to be invaded. If you have been assigned too many tasks that you cannot handle in the aftermath of your mother's death, speak up and do not neglect your instincts; if something does not feel right, it really is 't. Do not hesitate to ask for help.

If some of your relatives appear to be greedy because although rarely, this too can happen, try hiring a mediator to help distribute assets that have not been listed in the will. If the position of an executor has been given to you for the estate and you feel uncomfortable in this role, try hiring an independent fiduciary.

Similarly, if one of your siblings has been assigned this role and you feel like their judgment is greedy and unfair, take this route as well. You may also consider drawing names for items that have more than one sibling's interest. If you are feeling particularly tense around certain siblings, try to become more self-aware and analyze the situations in which you feel in a certain way. Try reflecting on these moments and if unmanageable, consider hiring a professional mediator. When it comes to money, real estate, and personal belongings, grief can bring out the worst in people. Make every effort to be kind and calm, but most importantly, look after yourself.

The anguish will eventually pass. Maintaining calm and focus makes things easier for everyone. the person's life has an impact on how they view their experiences. Grief is influenced by a variety of factors, including access to care, previous memories, resources, physical wellbeing, and self-doubt, both of which vary with age. As a result, when attempting to comprehend another person, it is normally beneficial to consider their stage of existence.

When you believe somebody is letting you down or doing things badly, it is tempting to lose faith in them; so before you pass judgment, remember all the things they have on their mind. besides dealing with the loss in itself, they may not have the time and needed support. Usually, family members try to do the right thing for their dead loved ones and carry out their wishes to the best of their abilities.

The truth is that people do not often go about telling their families and friends of their end-of-life desires. After certain topics have been explored, it is sometimes difficult to cover what you want to do with your most precious collections. With a lack of clarification, people are left speculating and, sadly, disagreeing about what the deceased person may have liked for their affairs and personal belongings. So, whether a will is in place or not, some decisions need to be taken, leaving room for conflict.

Remember that recovery takes time for everyone, and you can always repair and rebuild relations with your siblings, even if hurtful words were spoken at the funeral or after the loss. Everyone experiences a rollercoaster of emotions after the loss of a parent, so be prepared and respect how each siblings is feeling. Keep an eye out for one another, and do not forget to look after yourself. Be mindful of your parents' interests when it comes to legal and planning matters, and do not be afraid to remind your siblings of this if you feel like the way they are acting is not what Mother would have wanted.

Try not to let physical and financial problems get out of control because of your feelings. Show kindness to your siblings and be open about your own emotions. Take each phase one at a time and depend on one another for help. The light will burst through the clouds of sadness with time and grace, and you and your family will be able respect your parent's memories.

Chapter 3:
The Funeral

W hen a loved one passes, some families find it difficult to decide when to hold the funeral. Allowing yourself ample time to make a final decision allows you to create a more personal send-off farewell, while commemorating the deceased's life in a meaningful and unique manner. Setting a funeral date for a loved one can be influenced by a variety of factors, including religious beliefs and family circumstances.

The funeral is usually carried out between one to two weeks after the death. Some cultures and traditions even hold it up to three days after the death if there are no issues. If family members living abroad wish to attend, it could be delayed allowing people to travel to their home country. Funerals usually take place either in the morning or early afternoon, mostly on weekdays or on Saturdays. It is best to collectively choose a date and time convenient for all the family members. Everyone wants to pay tribute to their late mother, and they should be allowed to do so. Some decide on a date for the funeral by taking into consideration any special occasions such as birthdays. They would usually avoid holding a funeral on the same day and move it by a day or two.

If some of the family members happen to be abroad, make sure you let them know of the unfortunate event; and before setting up the funeral, allow enough time for them to return home from their trip. If the funeral is held on short notice, a lot of people may not attend. In Catholicism, the funeral is usually held two days after the death, and if cremation is an option, more time can be allowed before the ceremony is held. In the Jewish tradition, the funeral is held as quickly as possible following the death, and this may cause an issue for those who need to make travel arrangements.

Cremation is forbidden in Muslim burials, and the event usually takes place within 24 hours after death. Nonetheless, most religious communities are more flexible nowadays. The bottom line is that the method of burial has an impact on how soon the funeral is planned after death; preserving or cremating the body gives the grieving many more options. Besides traveling schedules, funeral home availability also affects when a funeral is held. Some Christian holidays are respected, and parish churches would not be available during days like Christmas and Easter Sunday. Budget is another factor that plays an important part in how a funeral is organized. Some may struggle to financially accommodate the wishes of the deceased, but a beautiful service can still be organized on a tight budget because what counts the most is the respect paid.

If your late mother was an organ donor, be prepared for the authorities to take her organs for preservation. After the loss, make sure you get the necessary documentation to organize a funeral, like death certificates; and if you are unable to organize a funeral in your current mental state, hire a funeral director. If your late mother was housed in a care home or nursing facility, you may be restricted as to how many days the deceased is kept in-house.

If your mother had insurance to cover funeral expenses, make sure you speak to the company and ask for assistance concerning any standard procedure to claim benefit. If you were given the rights to handle your mother's bank accounts during her last years, be advised that once she has been declared dead, her bank accounts will be frozen, and you may no longer be able to withdraw money to pay for expenses during and after the funeral. This is particularly useful information if you intend to use her money to pay for their funeral if this is something they wanted. There are different types of services but the main three are funeral, memorial, and graveside. A funeral is a service held before the body is buried. A memorial is service after the body is buried. A graveside is the funeral service that takes place at the gravesite.

Whichever service you chose, you need to arrange for a location, date, time, and budget. If death takes place away from the location you wish the service to be held, you must arrange for repatriation services. This can be very expensive; but if the deceased had insurance, the company can help with the planning. Some may opt for cremation in the country where the person died and have the ashes shipped. This can be more cost-effective and allows for flexibility when it comes to funeral services. It all depends on finances, religious beliefs as previously stated and, of course, the availability of the desired service at the location.

Together with the funeral, one needs to plan for cemetery arrangements, especially if the deceased had not already purchased a plot. If you belong to a religious community, they may help you find a vacant space. If you are working with a funeral director, they may also arrange this for you. Based on the community you belong to, you may need to plan for pre- and post-service events. A viewing, wake, or visitation are common pre-funeral events. Receptions or gatherings are common post-funeral events. If you follow religious traditions, these events may be influenced by them.

You may need to decide when and where your events take place. Although this may be something that loved one's struggle with, arrangement for how the body is prepared need to be made. Some may opt for an open casket because they feel it offers closure. Open-casket ceremonies require embalmment. Some religions prohibit embalming; therefore, an open-casket ceremony would not be possible. You must decide on what clothing you want your late mother to be buried in. You can opt for jewelry too.

If you are opting for cremation, remember to remove any jewelry from the body. Whether you opt for cremation or burial, you must choose the casket or the urn. If you wish to organize a funeral procession, you need to plan for transportation. Nonetheless, whether this is done or not, transportation still needs to be arranged to take the body to the funeral service and then to the graveside.

After arrangements for the funeral are made, you need to inform nonimmediate family members and friends. This can be done in many ways: newspaper, social media posts, emails to their address book, or by simply calling a key person who will then advise the rest. It is important to give all the necessary information: the dress code, date, time, location, and any parking available nearby.

If you are planning post-service events, make sure you let them know. Prepare a proper outfit to wear. If you wish to display photographs of your late mother, gather all you need. Make sure you have a guestbook if you want one and pens available. These little details would usually be taken care of by the funeral director if you hire one. During the service, you may need to select people to speak alongside the officiant, usually a religious leader if carried out in a religious institution. Speakers may not always accept your invitation, so make sure you have a few people to read. the funeral director arranges for pallbearers. If someone wishes to be a pallbearer but is physically incapable, they may walk by the casket instead of carrying it. You and your family members can agree on music, violinist or pianist, and readings for the service. You or the hired funeral director may also put together a funeral program listing the service, participants, and readings.

Every family and situation are unique; but planning and discussing the issue ahead of time when your family is healthy and not grieving the loss of a loved one can aid in deciding to honor and start celebrating your loved one's life in a dignified and positive manner. If you did not hire a funeral director, you may want to make decisions with your relatives. If some seem disinterested and discouraged to participate in the organization part, bear in mind that they may be struggling with the situation overall, and it is not because they could not care less.

Allow every immediate family member to pitch in their wishes for the funeral. If anyone wishes to express themselves but knows they may be overtaken by emotions, chose to read on their behalf. If you are the one struggling to read during the funeral but wish to have your piece read, ask another family member to read on your behalf. Accept that memorial services can be held in any way you want and that is not just one way. Do both if one sibling prefers a traditional service and the other prefers a celebration of life at Mom's favorite restaurant. Plan services around each other so that no one must choose between them and invite loved ones to say their goodbyes in any way they want. Make a plan that everyone can contribute to. Make concessions where you can but stand firm on what matters to you.

Chapter 4:
The Will

After someone passes, all their belongings are referred to as their estate. This includes money, whether cash or stored in the bank, shares, property, and any other personal possessions like jewelry and cars. If the deceased owes money, this should come out of their estate. In most cases, there would be a will in place, but if it were an unexpected and sudden death, it could be that the will is not yet in place. If this is the case, estates are divided according to the legal rules in that country.

If someone wrote a will, they would most probably have discussed it with relatives, but if you are unsure how to find the will, start by asking their solicitor or accountant.

The division of the estate is done according to intestacy rules. Under these regulations, married and civil partners and close relatives inherit the estate. Cohabiting partners are not legally eligible to inherit in cases where a will is not in effect. Children, grandchildren, and partners are all considered eligible candidates under intestacy law. Usually, after married or civil partners, children are next to inherit. If there is no surviving partner of the deceased, then the children would inherit everything. If there is more than one child, the estate is usually divided between them.

Inheritance is usually not handed to children until they reach the legal age, usually 18-years of age. There may be multiple versions of the will. Only the most recent one can count as valid, but do not destroy any previous versions. Copies of the will can be distributed among immediate family members, especially those entitled to the inheritance.

If a will has been set, someone has likely been appointed as the executor or administrator responsible for distributing the estate. The executor is in charge of collecting all legal documents belonging to the deceased. They are responsible for notifying all legal institutions and providing them with a death certificate to seize service: for example, for health insurances and financial institutions like banks. In this instance, bank accounts are seized, and insurance policies lapse. The administrator must open accounts solely used for the estate and find out details about the property and money owed. When inheriting, tax must usually be paid, depending upon the rules of the country. The administrator is responsible for calculating the tax due and distributing the amount between siblings. Possessions, debts, money, and property are listed so everyone is aware of the estate available. Debts and expenses are paid by the administrator, and the estate is then shared as stated in the will. Make sure that services such as telephone and TV are stopped. You must notify such companies of your mother's passing. If your late mother made use of a national health network, make sure you notify them of the death as well so they can update their records to avoid receiving correspondence in your mother's name for years down the line.

Before the inheritance is divided, make sure you contact the lenders if the deceased faced debt. If this happens after the assets are divided, you may have to pay the debt out of pocket. It is important to note whether the deceased had a payment protection insurance policy, usually taken up at the same time as a home loan or mortgage, to cover for such cases. In this instance, the remaining credit can be paid off by the insurance policy without affecting the estate left behind, consequently affecting the division between siblings. If the house to be inherited is subject to a mortgage, it may be that banks ask the new owner to settle the mortgage or take it over with the same terms if a protection insurance policy is not in place. If there is insurance as protection, the bank needs to open a claim with the company once you or your siblings notify them that the owner has passed.

You can be assigned the role of an executor but have every right to refuse. If no executor was mentioned in the will and you are a close relative of the deceased, you may apply to occupy the role. Legalities need to be satisfied that vary from country to country. Some families distribute the estate as instructed in the will with an executor in charge. Other cases are more complicated and may require a solicitor to step in, especially where the estate is complicated.

If the will is not clear or parts of the estate need to be passed on to someone under the legal age of 18 years, it is best to assign that distribution to a solicitor. If the deceased owns property outside the home country, her business, or the will distribution is likely to result in family feuds, you are better off hiring a solicitor. The legal fees associated with the solicitor can be paid out of the estate. If one of your siblings is assigned the role of the executor and is delaying distributing the assets or misusing the power assigned to them, look into hiring a solicitor. Documents usually required for sorting things out after the death of a relative include the will, birth certificate, death certificate, and marriage or civil partnership certificates if the deceased was married.

Managing a loved one's will after they die suddenly becomes difficult, especially if you are going through a tough time yourself. Estate distribution can be a challenging task, especially while grieving. Dividing estates create family conflicts and add to the stress. So, if you feel like you cannot execute the will, feel free to step out; and if you predict conflict, do not hesitate to suggest the help of a solicitor. Make sure everyone is involved in this sensitive process, without involving non-immediate family members to avoid further opinions and conflicts.

Chapter 5:
Turmoil of Emotions

W hen a mother of an adult dies, there is an unexpressed expectation that it will not hit you in the face. Adults are forced to embrace death as a natural fact of life and deal with all unexpected losses in a mature manner. But what exactly does that imply? Does it mean you are not supposed to be sad? Does it mean you should be thankful they did not die when you were a child and therefore you do not have to grieve? Grief is your way of reflecting on a now lost connection.

Today's society puts a lot of pressure on people to get over their losses and move on from grief. Do you feel less sorrow for your 50-year-old mother? The loss occurs in an instant, but the consequences last a lifetime. Grief is genuine because loss is sincere. Each loss leaves its mark as distinct and unique as the person lost. It makes no difference how old people are. You sometimes lose sight of how close you are to your parents. They are frequently your primary point of contact in and with the outside world. The belief that a mature and skillful adult does not need to grieve a parent can make the bereaved feel even more isolated as their grief goes unnoticed.

Right after the loss, you take your time to reflect on who your mother was, maybe even be the first time. You reflect on all the things your mom did for you as a kid. You start appreciating the challenges she went through to give you the best life had to offer. You now come to change the perception you had of your mother and the way you perceive life. As you grew, your relationship with your mother changed; and as an adult, you understood that they will be gone someday, and you are most likely going to live to remember it.

Right after the loss, you experience a mix of emotions, all associated with the connection you had with your mother and how you are grieving. You start to feel angry because your loss feels unfair. You start feeling angry because you would do anything to turn back time and change things or do things you wish you could have done. Because you cannot turn back time, you start to experience anger besides for the loss itself. You may experience different levels of anger; it may be inappropriate at times to lose control over otherwise trivial things. You may become angry at the doctors who treated your mother and may blame them for not being able to save someone who meant so much to you. You may blame it on the healthcare system or at yourself for not doing enough to save her, even if you know very well that this fell outside your capabilities.

You may feel angry for not spending enough time with her during her lifetime and not prioritizing her. Anger is proof that you are not insensitive, and your mother meant something to you. With this emotion, you may push away some of your closest family and friends, some of whom might be of great help during the grieving process.

Weeks or months later, you may start to experience symptoms of depression, and you start experiencing the loss on a deeper level. At this point, you may feel like you will remain like this forever. This stage is part of grieving, but in most cases it does not lead to a full-blown mental illness. Accepting the reality that your mother did not get better and cannot come back puts you in a very depressive stage. This stage after a loss is not permanent, but you must allow yourself to feel depressed. Depression helps you understand the real meaning of loss and what Mother meant to you. It allows you to redefine yourself from scratch. Depression can help you find yourself, something you did not do before because you had never allowed yourself to feel this way. You may also experience emotional numbness and shock from the tragic news. You may be in disbelief, feel confused, and experience a sense of unreality.

You may also feel hopeless and desperate. If you saw your mother suffering from a terminal illness, you may experience some level of relief because she doesn't have to suffer pain any longer. You may experience worry and wonder how you are going to cope without your mother in your life. You can no longer go on with life because things are going to be so different now that she is gone. You fear the moments you are going to miss and how the void she left behind can never be filled by any other presence. You may go back to conversations or moments you had with your late mother.

When someone you care about passes, it is as if you have been wounded by their death. Loss is frequently compared to an open, traumatic wound that must be healed. The pain of loss, like that of a physical injury, is intense at first. The wound is all you can think about; it consumes you, and any movement serves as a reminder of its presence. Although pain is not an emotion, but rather a sensation experienced by the body, it is something you feel after losing someone as precious as your mother. Pain is governed by all the emotions associated with loss like depression, anxiety, anger, and fear. One of the most challenging areas of being human is witnessing the agony of loss. When someone you love can no longer be a part of your life, the pain is excruciating, whether you are a child or an adult.

Chapter 6:
The Grief Process

G rief is most people's understanding of the complex pain that follows the death of a loved one. It is a natural reaction to a tragedy and involves both emotions and a physical reaction. This is experienced individually after an important relationship ends or the loss of a job. For the purpose of this book, the grief process is going to be explained as the death of a mother. Although grief is different for everyone, it is mainly divided into five to seven stages. This theory is based on a work published by Dr. Kubler-Ross in 1969 in Switzerland. The work was initially intended to study the grief process experienced by terminally ill people preparing for their death and focused on the five stages of grief. Because this theory was mainly based on people preparing to die, studies have enhanced the theory and added further stages.

This process involves a set of emotional responses used to heal and cope with this difficult time. The five stages process are just as good, but the following gives better insight into the feelings and processes experienced by those grieving the loss of a mother. For example: the stages of grief and loss help you understand and contextualize where you are in the grieving process and how you are feeling. Similarly, if you are worried about someone else's grieving process and want to learn more about it, keep in mind that there's no one-size-fits-all approach. Everyone grieves in their own way. You could experience a wide range of strong emotions or appear unaffected by them.

The amount of time spent going through the stages of grief differs from person to person. It could take you hours, months, or even years to process and heal from a loss. You may or may not go through all the stages of grief in the order listed. You could jump around from one stage to the next. You could even skip all these feelings and deal with your loss in a different way.

Stage 1 - Shock and Denial

Stage one of grief is denial in which you try to convince yourself that the loss did not happen. You begin to deny the facts, allowing you time to progressively accept and process the information. This is a common defence technique that helps you become numb to the situation's severity. Denial eventually entails denying one's suffering or sense of loss. For example, after the death of a loved one, you may act as if the loss is insignificant or has no impact on your daily life. This stage is a defence mechanism to help you buffer the shock and hurtful feelings. You might feel as if nothing matters to you anymore. The way you used to live has changed. It may be difficult to believe you are ready to move on.

This is a normal response that causes you to process your grief at your own pace. By becoming desensitized, you allow yourself to experience the changes you are experiencing at your own pace. Denial is a temporary coping mechanism that gets you through the first tide of discomfort. When you are ready, the emotions and feelings you have suppressed reappear, and your healing journey can continue.

Stage 2 - Pain and Guilt

You may believe that the loss is overwhelming and your thoughts and needs are making other people's lives more difficult. When the shock fades off, the sensation is replaced with unbearable pain. Even though the pain is almost debilitating, it is important that you truly feel rather than hide from, avoid, or escape it with alcohol or narcotics. During this time, life feels unpredictable and frightening. You are likely to feel sad, guilty, and desperate. You will feel discomfort after the shock has worn off and you realize the gravity of the situation. It is possible that the agony is unbearable, both physical and mental. Even if it is illogical, you might begin to feel bad about what you could have done for the person. It is natural to ask whether you should have done more to avert the tragedy or feel regret for not being able to come to terms with the loss of a loved one at this stage. While these feelings can be debilitating, they are the normal emotions associated with remorse, and acknowledging them as part of the healing process is vital.

Stage 3 - Anger and Bargaining

Pain takes many different forms. Loss-related pain is frequently diverted and conveyed as anger, according to Kübler-Ross. It is common to feel extremely angry, which may surprise you or your loved ones. This rage has a reason to exist. Anger can be particularly overwhelming for some because it is a feared or rejected emotion in many cultures. You may be more accustomed to avoiding than confronting it. During this stage, you start to ask "Why me?" and "What did I ever do to merit this?" or "Why did my mom have to leave this world?" You may become enraged at physical objects, strangers, friends, or family members without reason. You may be enraged by life itself. It is common to be angry at the situation or person you have lost. You might rationally conclude that the person is not to blame. However, you may despise them emotionally for inflicting pain or abandoning you.

You might feel guilty for being angry at some point, which could make you even more enraged. Remind yourself that your anger is fueled by pain. Even if it does not feel like it, anger is essential for healing. After separating yourself from the world during the denial phase, anger is a way to interact with it again. When you are numb, you are cut off from the rest of the world. However, anger is not the only emotion you might feel at this point. Other ways you might cope with your loss include mood swings, negativity, uneasiness, rage, and frustration. Everything is a part of the same process. During this stage, you take out your anger on others or even on yourself.

Anger is one of the most misinterpreted emotions, and many people are embarrassed by it. Surprisingly, anger can help you heal. It is a crucial stage in the grieving process. Getting rid of angry feelings relieves tension and affords a sense of regulation. When one loses a significant relationship, they feel helpless and impotent, so regaining control serves as a good reaffirmation that life goes on. Yelling into a pillow is a cliché for a reason; you should activate your anger in ways that will not damage others. But if you do lose your cool at a gathering, do not be too hard on yourself. No one is perfect; and if the people in your life are aware that you are grieving, they are more likely to be understanding.

Have you ever asked your higher power to change something that happened in your life if you pray? Maybe you offered to improve a particular aspect of your life in exchange for a specific result. This is a form of bargaining. In a situation of extreme pain, bargaining is a way to keep hope alive. You might think to yourself that if your life could be re-established like before the loss, you would be prepared to do and give up everything.

Guilt may accompany this stage because you are unknowingly attempting to regain control, even at your own cost. All these feelings and thoughts are not unusual. As difficult as it may seem, this could help you heal as you face the truth. Bargaining is the hope or belief that one set of conditions can be exchanged for another. You might want to undo something that has already happened. You understand this is not possible in cases of death, and bargaining brings up issues you would rather avoid. However, in the process, you are forced to admit that the event has occurred. By pleading with a higher power to bring someone back, you are implying that they are no longer alive. So, you are indirectly starting to accept the reality of the situation.

Stage 4 - Depression, Reflection, and Loneliness

You fully know the true extent of your loss at this moment, and it depresses you. You may want to isolate yourself on purpose, reflecting on things you did with your mom and focusing on memories. You may undergo a sense of emptiness or depression. Although depression after a loss is not always the same as clinical depression, the two types of persistent sadness have similar effects on people: sadness, frequent crying, loss of appetite, and sleep disturbances are all symptoms of depression. Aches and pains affect people. Your immune system deteriorates, as a result, making you more vulnerable to sickness. Grief-associated depression passes over time, while clinical depression does not and often evolves into a chronic condition that one needs to learn to live with by adopting coping techniques or treatment. You may be thinking about death or suicide if you feel the loss is the end of your life or you have lost your reason to live. Suicidal thoughts are not always about wanting to die; they can also be about wanting to cease your existence.

Suicidal ideation is when you wish to go to sleep and not wake up. If you are feeling like you do not have a reason to live, about dying, wanting to harm yourself or commit suicide, seek professional mental help immediately. See your family doctor as the first line of treatment; they may also be available to see you imminently. If your case is something they cannot handle, they may refer you to a psychiatrist.

Once you seek help, tell them what you have been through: you recently lost someone very dear to you, hence why you are feeling the way you are. This will help them assess your case accordingly. Depression, like the other stages of grief, manifests in a variety of ways. There is no such thing as a right or wrong method to go about it, and there is no time limit. Depression is not a sign of a mental health problem: it is a natural and healthy reaction to grief. During the depressive stage, you begin to confront your current circumstances and the inevitability of the loss suffered. Understandably, this realization may make you feel extremely sad and depressed. This deep sadness will make you feel differently in other ways as well. Depression can make you feel defenseless, lethargic, baffled, distracted, and unable to enjoy life.

This feeling may hit you in the morning. leaving you unable to get out of your bed. this is usually only temporary and a direct result of the grieving process. This stage, as difficult as it may seem, is an important part of healing.

Prolonged depression with feelings of guilt, confused speech, suicidal thoughts, and hallucinations may mean that your depression turned into major depressive disorder, especially if they occur years after the loss. If you are unable to continue with your day-to-day tasks long after the death of your mother, you may need to seek medical assistance. If you are unsure whether you are going through grief or depression, talk to your doctor or therapist; they can help you distinguish between the two. If your symptoms are related to normal bereavement, they will most likely improve over time.

Stage 5 - The Upward Turn

The phases of mourning, such as rage and suffering, have faded by this time, and you are left in a more peaceful and comfortable state. Your world gets a bit calmer and more orderly as you adapt to life without your mother. Your physical signs start to fade, and your sadness lifts IF marginally. You can start to see the light at the end of the tunnel at this point in the mourning process. It is a happy medium between all the mourning symptoms you have, and something to draw on. At this stage, you start feeling strengthened and motivated.

This stage feels like an awakening in comparison to the previous stages. Finally, as you think nothing positive can probably come your way again, you begin to feel a little better each day. It could be so trivial that you are unaware of it at first, and you may not be satisfied all at once. You may feel less discomfort, a little less depression, and a little more like yourself.

Stage 6 - Reconstruction and Working Through

Grief is an ongoing process. However, feeling anxious or depressed is not necessarily a part of it. A mourning person continues to work in the aftermath of death during the "reconstruction and working through" stage of grief. This stage is just as important as the others. However, it seems to take a different turn, as you start stop experiencing impending doom. Your mind begins to work again as you become more functional, and you may even find yourself finding practical solutions to challenges created by life without your loved one.

You focus on logistical and financial issues, as well as rebuilding yourself and your life in the absence of the loved one. You will start putting your life back together and moving on. During this stage, you start feeling inspired and determined. You may also feel refreshed at this point.

Stage 7 - Acceptance and Hope

Acceptance does not always imply agreement with what has occurred. It is comprehensible not to ever feel this way, depending upon your background. Acceptance is more about how you accept your misfortunes, learn to live with them, and adjust your life in response. During this time, you may feel more comfortable reaching out to friends and family, but you may also feel withdrawn at times. You may also feel as if you have accepted defeat before moving on to the next stage of grief. This back-

and-forth between stages is normal and necessary for healing.

You may find yourself for an extended period in the future. This does not mean you cannot be sad or angry about your loss in the future; it just means your long-term perception and how you deal with it can be different. You realize how important the loved one was to you. You've acknowledged the fact that you've suffered a tragedy and are no longer attempting to bargain it away. You can see a way forward in your life. It means you are aware of the situation's stability while continuing to live your life.

You have not forgotten about your loss, but it no longer consumes your thoughts every day. Most of the time, you are at ease in your acceptance. Acceptance is, in some ways, as painful as any other step in the grief process. Remember that accepting the reality of loss does not imply you will forget about your loved one. Memories of them will always be crucial, even if they are no longer the focus of your life. Given the agony and trauma you have been through, you can never be the carefree, unconcerned person you were before the crisis. You can, though, find a way forward and begin to anticipate and make plans. You now start to accept a new way of life without your loved one. Despite the fact that they are missing from your life, you can start feeling hopeful again.

Complicated Grief

The above stages are typically associated with grief as a standard process; however, not everyone goes through them. Some experience complicated grief. When abnormal, such grief over the loss of a loved one becomes severe and lasts much longer than it should. Complicated grief, also known as persistent complex bereavement disorder, can occur. Grief is a healthy and normal part of life, but it becomes abnormal when you are unable to function and the sad and painful emotions last for months or even years. Complicated grief is when someone remains grieving for longer than expected and shows no signs of recovering.

Symptoms of complicated grief:

- Prolonged disbelief of the death

- Inability to accept death

- Lengthy preoccupation of the loved one's death

- Prolonged emotional suffering and pain

- Unable to enjoy or recall good memories of the loved one

- Continuous to blame oneself for the loss

- Avoidance of reminders of the death

- Prolonged feelings of loneliness

- Prolonged feeling of emptiness

- Losing one's purpose in life after years following death

- Inability to carry out normal activities or complete daily tasks

- Isolation and withdrawal from social situations

- Suicidal thoughts, wishing you had died with your loved one

- Feeling of guilt about the death and wondering if there was anything you could have done

- Difficulty thinking about anything else besides your loss

If you were a caregiver to your sick mother, you may have started grieving her while still alive; this may lead to complicated grief too. If you do not have a strong support system or had a very close relationship with the deceased, you may experience it. If you've been depressed or had post-traumatic stress disorder (PTSD), you are more prone to it. If at the time of the loss you had been going through a difficult time such as financial trouble or were diagnosed with a chronic illness, you may be more prone to experience complicated grief.

It is understandable to experience grief for months and even years after the loss of someone as precious as your mother; however as time goes by, symptoms of grief should dimmish and are not meant to interfere with the activities of daily life, such as going to work, after one or two years. This isn't to suggest that you shouldn't experience complicated grief; but rather, identifying when this is the case and seeking assistance is key to understand why such emotions are still running so strong and how to overcome it to go back to participating in one's daily role as partners or parents.

The inability to move ahead after a decent length of time is the most revealing indicator of complex mourning. In general, grieving people go through the stages of mourning and embracing their loss, adjusting to life without the deceased, and developing a new connection or accepting the emptiness left behind in order to go on with their lives.

One may also display avoidance a and negative coping mechanism during grief. Experiential avoidance is a strategy for avoiding, minimizing, or changing painful memories, emotions, or bodily sensations. These are painful or threatening internal experiences that may include fear of losing control, embarrassment, or bodily injury, as well as thoughts and feelings such as embarrassment, guilt, despair, emptiness, separation, and seclusion.

People who don't like to experience painful feelings tend to avoid grief. Each new wave brings a sea of negative feelings, affirmations, emotions, and memories, which can be predictable in some cases while not in others. Many people may experience emotions of this magnitude for the first time; as a result, they may exhibit unsettling physical, behavioral, and emotional responses. This is particularly true for those who have not yet developed a solid set of coping skills. No experience in life helps you prepare for such a loss. Negative coping can go to the other extreme, where one turns to substance or alcohol abuse to avoid the pain.

Coping not only relates to the loss but also to change. It is natural to have a journey with your grief. It is not ideal to avoid pain or seek to stow your sorrow away. You must acknowledge that the loss has happened and is very real. It is perfectly fine to write your feelings down in a journal or avoid crowds for a while.

During grief, you may forget to do the most basic things, like taking care of your personal hygiene or getting enough sleep. This only deteriorates your mental health, especially if this behavior extends to years after the death. Getting over grief may feel as if one disconnects with one's late mother, but this is not the case. You can never fully disconnect because you have a physical connection. Although you prefer they were still around, you need to think of them to rekindle that connection. Getting through the process of grief to reach acceptance does not mean they are now eliminated from your life. In complicated cases of grief, this does not happen.

Grief is a part of life that everyone goes through when they lose someone they value, whether a loved one, job, or relationship. Because powerful sentiments of sorrow and loss are common and natural, they are rarely identified in the same way that illnesses like anxiety or depression are. You may adopt efforts to assist in coping with your loss. You may be overtaken by loss at first, but your life ultimately adapts and expands around it.

Grief alters you and the way you see things, so you never move on. Grief finally makes you stronger and wiser. Things you avoided doing while mourning, such as socializing and committing to your job, are eventually reintroduced into your life. You learn to cope with loss and though you never forget your late mother, you do not let it control your life.

Chapter 7:
Grief and Anxiety

Anxiety is a common side effect of mourning, but if your symptoms persist six months after a loved one has died, you may be suffering from complicated grief or an anxiety disorder. Anxiety is not one of the grieving stages, although many specialists in the field feel like it should be. When you lose a loved one, the aftermath can be paralyzing. People who are grieving often feel as if they have lost their sense of security and control in life, and they begin to panic or worry obscenely about what or who they might lose in the future. They may also have difficulty sleeping or caring for themselves, putting them at risk for anxiety.

Aside from death, secondary losses such as financial or emotional support can have an impact on mental health. Anxiety is a normal and expected part of the grieving process, but people who suffer from complicated grief are more likely to develop anxiety disorder. Complicated grief, often linked to an anxiety disorder, is defined as intense grief symptoms that interfere with daily life and occur more than six months after a loss. This link is reciprocal, as people who have an anxiety disorder may be more likely to experience complicated grief when they lose a loved one. If your initial feelings of anxiety after a loss do not go away, you may be suffering from anxiety disorder. An anxiety disorder manifests itself as:

- Excessive worry, restlessness, and fatigue

- Irritability and difficulty concentrating

- Sleep disruption

- Specific phobias and muscle tension

- Social phobia

- Irregular heartbeat

- Light-headedness and dizziness

- Breathing problems

- Nausea and suffocation

- Perspiring and shivering

- Sudden chills or hot flashes

- Feelings of tingling in your limbs

- Worry that you are going insane

- Fear of dying or becoming seriously ill

People experiencing anxiety because of a loss may also experience panic attacks. If you become dizzy, experience chest pain, or have a feeling of choking, speak to your doctor. While it is natural to feel fear and apprehension during times of adversity and high stress, if you are concerned about excessive worry and fear in the absence of a real threat for an extended period, seek help from a mental health professional.

Even if you try your hardest to prepare for loss, there is only so much you can do for the mental and emotional effects of grief, especially when the "seven stages" you have learned to expect to feel seem incomplete. When you come to terms with reality by understand that you are not in control of everything that happens in your life, you may become anxious about losing someone else in or experience similar pain in the future. All these emotions and fears may seem strange and overwhelming at first. Many people do not realize the link between grief and anxiety until they are in desperate need of assistance.

You may not experience anxiety right after the loss. The fact that the immediate aftermath of a loss can be surprisingly busy is one possible reason why these anxious feelings do not usually surface until later. Making funeral arrangements, filling out paperwork, and tying up loose ends keep you distracted, making it easier to postpone the burden of grief until after those tasks are completed a few weeks later.

Symptoms such as chest tightness, irregular sleeping patterns, difficulty focusing, sudden crying episodes, and changes in appetite may start around that time. You might also have a general sense of helplessness or foreboding about the future. PTSD is more likely to manifest later in life than in the immediate aftermath of a loved one's death. Above all, do not put any pressure on yourself to feel that way by a specific date. Grief comes in cycles, and it is difficult to predict when it will strike.

You must understand how anxiety works and why you are feeling this way right now. Death and loss stimulate the fear-responders that place you on high alert and heighten physical stimuli. It helps you stay calm if you remind yourself that this is a natural response and your body's way of coping with stress. Check in with your grief and identify that a huge part of your life has gone missing, and you must learn to deal with this. If you feel like opening up about your regret to seek forgiveness, do so to ease the feeling of guilt. Understand that your intentions are not to move on but to become resilient and build a significant life around the loss.

You may work with a therapist to deal with the anxiety associated with grief but writing down your emotions can greatly help this phase as well. Cognitive-behavioral therapy (CBT) is an important part of overcoming grief-related anxiety. You may need to understand how grief affects the brain. This will be discussed later in the book, so stick around.

Try meditation to combat anxiety and free yourself from the racing thoughts in your head, related to your dear mother. This helps you develop a healthy spiritual relationship with your lost mother. In return, it can bring you peace and compassion toward what you are experiencing. You may start worrying about your death because you have been brought so close to this phase of life. If you start feeling anxious, try putting your affairs in order, like making a will if one is not in effect.

While it's important not to rush the grieving process, there is assistance and support available to help you regain control, manage the symptoms, and calm anxious thoughts. Anxiety can be treated with medication, counseling, or a combination of the two. Counseling can teach you how to reframe negative thoughts and interrupt harmful behavior, as well provide coping skills for anxiety.

Things cannot be the same as before the loss; but with time, you can feel more like yourself. Know if you're having a tough day that while you will always miss the person who died, you can find happiness again. It is natural for anyone to be afraid of death. Because losing someone you love puts you in a vulnerable position, you experience anxiety after a loss.

Our daily lives are altered after a loss. It makes you face your mortality and confronting these basic human truths about life's unpredictability can bring fear and anxiety to the surface in unforeseen and significant ways. Anxiety that arises after losing someone close to you is a distinct kind. While many of the symptoms of grief anxiety are like those of generalized anxiety, there is an underlying relational cause. As a result, we are better able to ease and manage the type of anxiety that comes with loss when we allow ourselves to grieve and truly explore its impact.

Chapter 8:
Grief and Relationships

T he grieving process is a deeply personal one. Because grief is such a personal experience, each person's reaction to the death of a loved one is unique. One spouse's instinct may be to reach out and connect with the other. Another partner may withdraw, become preoccupied with work or hobbies, or stop functioning. Your bond with the deceased was one-of-a-kind. As a result, the way you grieve will be unique and personal to you. Close friends and family you would expect to be there during one of life's most trying times may not be in the way you wish or expect.

Grief affects you and your relationship. It is frustrating and hurtful to have what appears to be a breakdown in your relationships just when you need them the most. However, keep in mind that grief is most likely affecting your friends, family, and spouse as well. They are grieving in their own ways; it just appears to be different from yours. It's also crucial not to put all your confidence in your partner. If you have other people to turn to for help, it can be healthier for both of you and should reduce the stress on your marriage. Grief puts a huge strain on existing relationships because it changes who you are as a person while you try to cope with the loss and find a way to move forward.

Close friends and family members may be unable to cope with your grief, causing them to withdraw temporarily. They may be accustomed to seeing you as a symbol of strength, and seeing you in this precarious position, on top of possibly dealing with their grief, maybe too much to endure.

Relationships take effort to maintain, and they are vulnerable to the challenges you face as you go through life. To find solace and understanding, you may need to turn to distant family members, other friends, or acquaintances, form new connections through bereavement groups, or seek professional help from a mental health counselor. Although bereavement can alter our relationships, one can expect some semblance of normalcy as everyone affected copes with the loss over time.

You can re-establish lost connections by forgiving friends or loved ones who were not there for you as you dealt with your grief the way you had hoped. Although everyone's grief is different, you and your partner can get on the same page and support each other. Couples or marital counseling may help you reconnect with your spouse or partner if you are having trouble as you grieve and need understanding and guidance.

Whether you have been around each other for a year or twenty years, you have probably experienced a personal tragedy that has affected both you and your partner at some point. These can range from minor troubles, such as failing to get that promotion at work, to major troubles such as a life-altering accident or the death of a loved one. These tragedies can be a test for relationships, especially if they occur at the beginning of one.

Couples learn to grow together and support each other in the most challenging times. Even when one is going through a tragedy, how couples support each other reveals a lot about their character and how they value the feelings of the other. When major tragedies occur, they have the potential to alter one's life and relationships. Being patient can be difficult. If your grief lasts much longer or is much more intense than you had anticipated, you may feel unable to support your partner.

Guilt arises when you are working to support a grieving partner, not only because you're finding it hard to get things right but also because you're finding things frustrating. Things will never be the same for each person and the relationship after a horrific accident, a family death, or other type of loss. The most important thing is that you and your partner get through it together. Support and love one another. You never know what's in store, but if you're there for each other, you are able to depend on each other and get through it.

It is critical to recognize and accept that everyone grieves in different ways. It is natural and expected to experience a spectrum of emotions in entire families or cultures. In some cultures, for example, it is customary for families to openly cry and spend as much time as possible at a funeral, grieving a loved one who has passed. Other cultures express their grief more privately. Even within the same household, each partner may be unique. One person may not want to cry openly or talk about the tragedy at all, while the other may want to talk about it all the time. No set of rules define how things should be done. They are just not the same.

The difficult part comes when both partners are grieving for the same tragedy in unique ways. Find a way to support your spouse in the way he or she needs to grieve, while also allowing yourself to grieve. Try to come to a compromise so you can share your reactions. It is fine to grieve in the way your family or culture does, and it is also fine to change your grieving style. Grief is neither good nor bad.

Allow your companion to express their grief at their own pace and encourage them to heal. Grief can take a long time to heal after a loss. Some people seem to get over it quickly, while others' grief lasts longer. Try not to be angry or resentful if one person is still grieving while the other does not appear to be. It does not imply that someone is stronger or weaker simply because they took less or more time. Grief has no time limit. It can last for years and triggered by both obvious and less obvious events.

If one partner tries to accelerate the grieving process, the relationship may suffer. During a tragedy, the two most important things you can do for your partner are to listen and love them – whatever you can do to alleviate the distress. You can be present, if nothing else, even if it is just to hold each other. Listening without judgment can be required almost daily. During the grieving process, it is normal for each partner to experience anger, frustration, a low mood, a loss of interest in daily activities, and other emotions.

Try not to take your partner's rage personally when he or she directs it at you. Possibly, they were not taught how to deal with it healthily. Simply pay attention and hold them. Assist them in directing their rage in a different direction, where it will not hurt you. Keep in mind that anger is a natural reaction to grief, so this is expected. Apart from being present, the most important thing anyone can do is maintain hope.

A person who has experienced tragedy may begin to believe that all hope has been lost and nothing is worth doing. It can descend into a downward spiral of negativity that is difficult to break free from. Always pay attention to their concerns while also offering hope. Hope eventually brings recovery. Unfortunately, when tragedy strikes, couples can become estranged. They allow big and small things to get in the way. Perhaps they want to grieve alone, or life has become too difficult for them to deal with, and they have simply stopped communicating.

If this goes on for years, there may be no connection or routes for communication anymore. Keep in mind that you have no control over how your partner acts. If your partner chooses to grieve separately, give them space while keeping the door open for them to return. It could be a difficult time for both of you if your partner decides that the marriage cannot work in their new life after a tragedy. Try to work your way through it and exhaust all possibilities. Never lose hope.

If you or your partner has developed anxiety, depression, or any other mental health issue because of a traumatic event, see a therapist. Go to relationship counseling if the tragedy is causing problems in the relationship, and you do not know how to fix them. Relationship therapy is essentially a means for assisting people in resolving conflicts and moving forward. It can assist in positively dealing with tragedy, provide tools to assist in dealing with it in everyday life, and provide advice for partners on how to provide support for each other. Many counselors are trained to assist with the impact of grief on relationships, while specialist grief counselors can provide one-on-one support.

It is sometimes easier to talk things over with someone who is not involved in the situation and can provide an objective perspective. Regularly checking in with your partner to see how they are doing and how you can help is one way to simplify things. While grief is a complicated process, it is like the many other things that challenge relationships in that it can be made easier by effective communication.

One partner may choose to maintain safe distance. The danger comes if they do not feel able to express what is bothering them, and the distance comes across as negligence or disinterest. It is far preferable to discover that the person does not require assistance by asking directly rather than discovering later that they could not express it at the time.

Similarly, if you belong to a faith-based group, you might find support and comfort there. Working with these resources can help not only with your recovery but also with forgiving those who were unable to support you during your grief. Take care of your body. If you are up to engaging in sexual activity with your partner, do so and take care of your relationship.

Sex is a life-affirming experience. In the best of times, sex can be a difficult topic for couples to discuss. Sex can make you feel vulnerable and feeling vulnerable may be too difficult for you while grieving. Stay in the moment and talk to your partner about it. Drink plenty of water and eat healthy foods. Of note, exercise regularly.

Anyone can be affected by a loss. It gives your relationship a new dynamic. You might feel as if you had a life before, and now you have a different one. Offering support is the only thing you can do for one another. Seek the assistance you require to keep the momentum going. Know that healing is possible as you adjust to your new normal.

Remember that you cannot put a time limit on grieving and subsequent healing. Your method is unique to you. Honoring this rule can serve as a model for others and lay the groundwork for future endeavors. Allow yourself to stop grieving for a while; a movie night with your partner does not imply disrespecting your late mother.

Chapter 9:
Grief and Work Performance

Many months after a loved one's death, a grieving co-worker who appears to be coping well may break down in tears during a meeting. During the early stages of grief, many people find it difficult to work. Take as much time as you need before returning to work, if possible. Someone grieving may have trouble concentrating at work and lack motivation.

If they hold a managerial position, they may struggle to make business decisions. They may lack energy and change their eating or sleeping habits. If the office regularly holds social events, they may withdraw from them while grieving. Because they are going through emotional turmoil that also affects them physically, they may be more prone to illness, thus calling in sick more often than usual.

If you recently lost someone as dear to you as your mother, make sure you tell your managers about the loss and ask them to share the information with the rest of the company if need be. Some departments choose to inform the entire company or limit the telling only your department. You may use social media to inform your closest friends and co-workers about the loss. Some turn to social media to let others know of the funeral so interested co-workers can attend. Your manager or supervisor may attend on behalf of the department, as it can be quite difficult to have an entire department attend especially if the funeral is during working hours.

If you decide to communicate this terrible news personally to your department, you may get co-workers to take some of your usual tasks to help alleviate the pressure; do not hesitate to accept this help. Bereavement leave is part of the entitlements at most companies so check with your manager or HR department. You may have a three-day entitlement, depending upon the country. Do not hesitate to ask for this leave. This is usually allocated if an immediate family member passes, such as a mother.

If you need additional leave, speak to your superiors to make all the necessary arrangements. If you feel you can get back to work but would prefer working from home to avoid the dynamics at the office, speak to your manager to see if this is a possibility. Some feel that returning to work as early as possible will help them get their mind off the loss focus on work-related duties. Despite your best efforts, your grief will tap you on the shoulder when you least expect it and trigger sadness and even tears in the workplace, no matter how much you hope that returning to work will distract you from your painful thoughts and feelings for a few hours.

If you feel there is a right time for this, meet your co-workers outside of work for lunch or dinner to accept their condolences outside the work environment. If your co-workers offer help with chores, childcare, or food preparation, accept it if you feel like this helping hand might ease your current struggle. Do not hesitate to ask for fewer tasks as you slowly get back to the office and take on your usual routine. You will not be able to predict everything that will trigger your grief once you return to work, so prepare for the times when your loss-response could get in the way of how you want to act.

Ask for space if you feel it's better to spend your lunch break in private instead of with the rest of the office. Allowing yourself to be sad and even cry when you are grieving is perfectly normal and natural, so instead of fighting it, prepare for it. Know that you can leave the office if you feel overwhelmed or advise your co-workers that you may spend more time than expected at the restroom because you need to be alone. If you are struggling to remember things because you are more distracted now, ask your co-workers to send you emails instead of verbally discussing work-related issues.

Try to avoid making big work-related decisions after your mother's death. It can take from up to a few months, and in some cases, up to a year. Big decisions can be influenced by the grief process you are experiencing, and you may regret them later. People are sincerely sorry for your loss and are doing their best to express their condolences. Some co-workers may be uneasy with loss or expressing grief if they appear detached or uninterested.

Recognize that you are not to blame for their discomfort. They mean well. They may avoid recognizing your emotions but do not ignore your own. Bringing a photo of the person who died to work, or purposefully using the person's name in conversation, is another way to express your grief. If you feel you need financial aid or advice, ask HR for help, as they may have programs in place designed to help employees in times of difficulty.

Supporting a co-worker who is grieving

Many people are afraid of saying the wrong thing or are so afraid of death that they avoid talking to someone who has lost a loved one. A personal call or note, as well as office-wide memorial contributions, cards, or flowers are appropriate ways to express sympathy. It is critical to acknowledge the loss and coordinate a company-wide response. Employees are aware of and grateful for this welfare. After a significant loss, shock and numbness are common reactions. Grief brings with it screw-ups, ambiguity, and an inability to concentrate.

Despite the numerous practical ways in which people can assist someone grieving a death, most people simply do not know how to console the bereaved, so they unknowingly distance themselves. You should be expected to daydream or commit a higher rate of inaccuracies upon your return to work if you have recently lost your mother. You may feel exhausted or sleepy during the day and may benefit from some flexible hours at work. Employees benefit greatly from strong time-off policies, sensitive managers, and open conversations during a time of bereavement. When a person is grieving, managers who build a trusting relationship can be a pillar in the recovery. Demonstrate that you understand their loss and inquire about what they would like you to tell others at work.

Sending flowers or a card is a generous act, and you could also ask if attending the memorial service would be appreciated. Work can be a life jacket for a familiar structure and choice in a time when life feels like an abyss. Some yearn to return to work as a distraction from their grief, as a reminder that there is one aspect of their lives over which they still have some control. Others may require more time, either for practical reasons or because their grief is more overwhelming.

Some employees may wish to bring some of their grief to work in the hopes that it will be recognized by others. People begin to act on their desire for deeper relationships, real conversations, and meaningful work if they are given the space and authorization to do so. With enough support, they eventually scrape up the courage to speak openly about how they have grown because of their loss.

If someone at work who you know shares a special connection with the bereaved, make sure you let them know that you are available to talk about their grief, easing their transition to the usual office schedule. It may help to reassign tasks or projects to someone else for a short period; and if their grieving is taking longer than planned, emphasize their responsibilities without adding too much pressure. If the bereaved seems to be avoiding large corporate events, try inviting them to smaller gatherings to make sure they feel your warm and welcoming environment and start easing into the larger events slowly.

If the company offers voluntary leave, try organizing voluntary activities like building a refugee home or help in an animal shelter. This can help the bereaved feel needed and give them their time off from the grief. Some grief experts acknowledge that the average bereavement allotted to each employee for immediate family members can be between three to four days; however, they acknowledge that such leave should be extended to twenty days.

Some may require bereavement leave for non-immediate family members' deaths because they have a close relationship with them. Returning to work three to four days after the death of a parent, spouse, child, cousin, or close friend can be difficult, regardless of who died. Most people are too preoccupied with planning services and calling family and friends to take the time to process their emotions. Keep track of the date and time of the funeral, as well as whether the employee would be traveling to attend. Avoid contacting the employee during these times, and request that the employee's manager do the same.

Some companies have a banking leave policy where other co-workers may donate a day of their own vacations leave to those that need it. This is particularly beneficial for those who do not have enough bereavement leave and wish to do a gesture of goodwill with their co-workers. If you have a multicultural office, make sure you understand the culture of the bereaved as it may be different than yours. Most importantly, if you notice self-destructive behavior from the bereaved, make sure help is arranged before their situations worsen.

Managerial support for grieving employees

Managers should be available to assist workers by controlling the workplace-employee boundary. Close co-workers are likely to reach out to grieving co-workers, but a manager must do so as well. Managers reflect the business, and their show of support sends a message that the company cares. A manager's appearance, whether through a call or a personal visit, goes a long way toward assuring employees that they are valued and supported. Do not be afraid to tell the bereaved what the policy is for going back to work and whether it is flexible while reassuring them that their co-workers are happy to see them when they do.

While some managers may find discussing an employee's return to work in the immediate aftermath of death unpleasant, the bereaved often craves clarity. When the employee is prepared to come to work, managers play a critical role in preparing co-workers by communicating the returning employee's wishes and possibly hosting a grief-recovery workshop led by an expert.

Allow grieving employees to make their own decisions and respect their choices. If they are unsure, give them some time. Inconsistency, as well as a lack of energy for challenges and improvement, are common after a loss. Neither is an indication that an employee's skill or passion for the job has subsided. Recognizing and managing these behaviors can help avoid miscommunication and disputes. Flexibility can benefit the bereaved from the structure of going back to work without feeling overwhelmed. If an employee is still having trouble several months after a loss, a manager may gently suggest that he or she seek professional help. Employee assistance programs at many companies include funding for short-term counseling, which can be helpful during the early stages of grief.

Six months after a loss, the inability to maintain regular work duties may be a symptom of complicated grief, which is distinct from the normal grieving process and necessitates clinical attention and, in some cases, medical leave. Managers who impress employees with a hopeful vision of the future are not the most helpful. There are those who pay attention and encourage them as they forge a new path forward, carving out space for the present-day. Not every manager can do this, but its works in small offices where the employees are closely knit and support a family-like environment.

Of course, not every manager will have had a major loss to turn into an interpretation of empathy. Even if they have not experienced bereavement, they are likely to have gone through difficult times and can draw on those experiences to create a comfortable environment for the bereaved. Managers help mourning employees by being present in moments of loss, patient with the inconsistency it causes, and open to its growth potential. They also complement what we expect from managers in terms of vision, planning, and assistance. Managers assist organizations in improving their performance by confronting grief. If the company offers free healthcare insurance coverage, it would be an additional benefit for company HR managers to include benefits in the policy such as therapy or counseling as part of the eligible treatment, if it is not already included.

While you do not want to step in and tell the bereaved what to do, understanding what grief is and how to help them can be beneficial to both the grieving person and those around them at work. The truth is that many people's grief intensifies after the funeral, memorial, or interment services have concluded, which is often around the time you need to return to work or the office.

For weeks or even months after a loss, a grieving co-worker may not be fully functional, and productivity may be below normal. Remember that while death and loss are difficult to talk about, confronting the grief can help you and your team get through these trying times.

Inquire with the co-worker about what you can do to alleviate some of the work stress he or she is experiencing. Again, communicating with your supervisor and co-workers can be crucial at this time to help them better understand what you are going through as well as to clear up any misunderstandings about your recent performance or potential resentment among co-workers who feel they must pick up your slack. For now, don't be too harsh on yourself because things will get easier over time.

Chapter 10:
Grief and Socializing

I t can feel as if the world has ended when you lose a loved one. The grief of losing a loved one, regardless of the circumstances, can be overwhelming and all-consuming. Each situation and each person's reaction will be distinct.

You may be too preoccupied in the days, weeks, or months following the death of your mother to consider the long-term implications of the changes in your circumstances. Do not be concerned if you feel fine one minute and helpless the next; this is completely normal and part of the grieving process. The first Christmas, birthday, or Mother's Day can be the most difficult to deal with. It is natural to want to stay in and avoid social situations after losing someone.

It is also normal if you want to socialize, but it feels awful once you are out and about. You may feel like the world goes on without you, but you are not a part of it. Similarly, you may not want to visit places or speak with people who had a relationship with your mother. Friendship is good for us, according to numerous scientific studies. Having strong social connections can help protect you from depression and stress. Friendships can be difficult to maintain after a loss, but they should become an important part of your grieving process over time. Friends may drift away if you never get out there, refuse offers, or stop speaking to those around you.

You may want to isolate yourself but socializing with people you know can put you in touch, no matter how difficult it is. You may find that you want to go out and socialize again in the future. Taking those first steps, however, can be intimidating if you have not socialized in a while. You might be hesitant to go out because you believe your friends have moved on. After you have given yourself time to grieve, decide to do things you enjoy, either with others or alone.

Join social clubs, take vacations, and submerge yourself in life and what is going on around you. If large groups of people or events are too much to handle at first, ask close friends to meet for small catchups. If you feel like you are not expressing your emotions and bereavement because your siblings are avoiding the topic, join a group. You can also opt for video calls or a simple telephone call that may take up hours of talking if you feel comfortable. If you find yourself feeling depressed, getting ready to go out can be a challenge, so this is a good alternative while still maintaining connections.

Just because you do not grieve in the same way or for the same amount of time as other people you know does not mean your grieving is not valid. Do seek support from friends and close co-workers, especially if you feel comfortable with your circle. Although you may not recognize it initially, your friends can help you overcome this difficult phase in life.

Chapter 11:
Bereavement and Young Adults

Many youngsters experience the death of a loved one during their early years, and it becomes part of growing up. This loss can be very disruptive for their growth and development, especially if they lose someone as close as their mother. Bereavement is a common life-defining experience a lot of young people go through.

Studies confirm that young people who live in disadvantaged environments are more prone to experience multiple losses at young ages. Young people who experience a loss and face other difficulties are prone to face limitations in school, have problems with self-esteem, and develop daring behaviors. A lot of youngsters who experienced losing their mother confess they never talked about it to anyone until a later stage in their lives, if at all.

Bereavement can disrupt their transition into social life and the development of emotions, making them more vulnerable. Adults frequently want to keep children in the dark about what is going on. Children, on the other hand, are more likely to spot that something is wrong and become anxious and confused if it is not addressed. They may prefer to know what is going on because grief affects them differently than it does adults.

Children, more so than adults, swing back and forth between grieving and going about their daily lives. They can be upset one moment and then demand to play football or eat ice cream the next. It is sometimes referred to as "puddle jumping," because the puddle represents their grief, and they move quickly in and out of it. They may return to the topic and ask you the same questions multiple times.

Alternatively, if they believe it bothers you, they may try to avoid mentioning the person. You can reassure them that talking is fine and, ideally, they will not keep their worries to themselves. Adolescents usually have a better understanding of death and consider how it could affect their lives in the long run. They may be more concerned about disruptions in their routines, such as who would look after them or the house. They might be concerned about money or the future. Their reactions can be difficult, and to talk about their feelings would be a struggle.

They would rather talk to their friends instead of the adults in their lives. They may also feel sad, angry, and guilty. Their emotions can be quite intense at times. The death may affect their performance at school or work if they already have a summer job or volunteer. They may wonder why this has happened. Bereavement can have psychological impacts, where it poses difficulty concerning development. It can also have a sociological impact, where weaknesses develop in institutional areas of life, leaving them relatively powerless.

While bereavement is an inevitable part of growing up, for some young people, it is a life-changing event with far-reaching implications short and long term. Very little research has asked young people to speak about their bereavement experiences. Consequently, when it comes to bereavement as a general feature of young people's lives, very little is known. They may struggle for years in the aftermath of a significant loss in ways that go unnoticed by those around them.

The idea that young people can get over death because they have a whole life in front of them is very inadequate. They may never get over it and revisit the experience at any stage of life. Youngsters who have lost their mothers may face difficulties handling overwhelming feelings, risk solation and a lack decision-making skills, with negative implications for their social lives. Some youngsters confess to developing higher self-esteem and finding their strengths. However, studies confirm that youngsters struggle with motivation and overwhelm. Multiple losses or difficulties, on the other hand, are strongly linked to an increased risk of adverse outcomes.

Multiple losses, in turn, are likely to be linked to social class, geopolitics, and general drawbacks. Families and friends of the bereaved may be struggling with their high levels of difficulty. Teenagers are required to learn to assume responsibility for and manage their public and private behaviors and emotions. This can make bereavement particularly difficult for children at a certain age, especially in educational settings.

According to some studies, many bereaved young people never speak to anyone about their feelings, and there is a risk of social isolation over time. Peers and family members of these young people can have very different relationships with them: they can be key sources of support or cause additional problems if the assistance they provide comes across as control rather than support. There may be additional issues between family members during a time of major crisis caused by bereavement.

Mutual protection or specific expectations of appropriate behaviors or responses imposed by more powerful family members are examples. Young people who are bereaved may also find their families to be hostile or abusive. Evidence suggests that policies should be aimed at enabling young people, their families, and communities, as well as the general professionals who interact with them to respond to bereaved young people.

As a society, one must recognize that bereavement is a common occurrence in most young people's lives, rather than viewing bereavement as a problem that only experts can solve. This should be a compelling argument for death education in schools. Peer support groups whether based in schools or bereavement organizations may be particularly effective when dealing with bereavement issues, as well as other issues that arise in the lives of young people.

There is very little research on how young people can get help or services for themselves, whether they have already contacted bereavement organizations or not. This is related to a broader set of issues involving health education and personal assistance for young people in general.

Bereavement must be included and given proper consideration in such broad areas of policy development as it is a potentially significant and difficult issue for young people. At the same time, policies must pay special attention to how to make bereavement support available to those who live in deprived and disadvantaged areas. These are the areas where sudden deaths are most likely to put young people at risk.

While research shows that a variety of services should be available to all, there is also a case to be made for paying special attention to troubled young people who may have experienced significant bereavement earlier in their lives, as well as bereaved young people living in disadvantaged communities. The young bereaved should be aided to accept the reality of their grief and allow their grief to work and progress while they continue to progress in their lives.

Teenagers grieve differently than adults. Although there is a standard model in place for how grief is usually experienced, there is no guide for how teenagers should go through grief. Adults can best assist grieving teenagers by taking on the role of listeners and allowing them to be the teachers of their own lives.

Responses to grief can vary from positive ones, where teenagers seek shelter in counseling and express their emotions with close friends. Grief can lead to drinking, taking drugs, and other self-destructive behaviors, which teens are more likely to experience than adults. Teens are particularly vulnerable because they lack the coping skills that many adults acquire over time.

As a parent, it is critical to be on the lookout for signs that your teen is using substances to cope. Your teen may also engage in risky sexual behavior, drop out of school, or engage in other behaviors that appear to be unrelated to the grieving process. These symptoms can indicate depression or anxiety, so keep the lines of communication open with your teen to help figure out what is going on.

Youngsters can react to grief in different ways based on their relationship with the deceased and according to their personalities. At a certain age, teenagers may be more affected by a death of a boyfriend or girlfriend and less affected by the death of a grandparent, depending upon the relationship held. However, the loss of a mother is always highly moving whatever the age.

The grieving process in teenagers is affected by the available support system, the circumstances of the death, whether the teenager had contact with the dead body, their relationship with the deceased, the teenager's involvement in the death (in cases where the mother was terminally ill), the emotional development of the teen (depending upon their age) and their previous experience with death - if they had any. Many teenagers express grief as a constant shift of ocean tides, sometimes calm and sometimes not.

The death of a parent can be devastating for a teen. The death can disrupt their lives and create complications. They may feel different than their peers, especially if schools celebrate Mother's Day or Woman's Day. They may feel a void all year round but especially on these occasions. The death may define their teenage years, and they start referring to their life as before and after the death. If their relationship with their mother was a conflictual one, they may either experience guilt or relief following the death.

Because as teenagers, they would still be financially dependent, the loss of a parent can seriously affect their stability. The other parent, if present, may help by discussing the options and give a realistic picture of the financial situation so that teenagers and parents will feel some sort of stability. When it comes to filling the void during special occasions with the remaining parent, such occasions may not be easy, but celebrations can be used to memorialize the deceased.

Teens may also worry about their living parent both because they fear losing them if they fall ill or feel lonely. The remaining parent may impose difficult responsibilities like running errands and taking care of the house on top of the duties teenagers already have like completing their studies. Teenagers may take over the role of the missing parent voluntarily or unknowingly. If their mother passed due to a chronic illness, teenagers may fear their death and are scared that they may also have the same disease, especially if it is highly hereditary.

Adolescents may struggle with grief because they have developed an attachment with the deceased; and once they pass away may want to form alternative attachments. While adults too have attachments, youngsters are more dependent on them and may seek to recreate them with other people who in most cases are their same age with very little experience of death.

Attachments in youngsters may only be appreciated when they end, leaving behind a huge deal of guilt and the feeling of a void. For teenagers to be aided through their grief, a therapist, or a school counselor must understand the attachment the young adult had with their late mother. This is mostly done through active listening.

In cases of young children, play therapy may also be used. The mode of death is very important for young adults because this may raise concerns, especially if they encountered a dead body or witnessed suffering in before their mother passed. Through active listening, one should identify sources of stress and grief and learn how to deal with stressors with the young adult. They must learn skills to deal with them, while always remembering the nice memories they lived had of the deceased. In short, they do not let grief control their lives. Skills would ideally be constructive coping techniques in the form of small improvements that eventually lead to long-term benefits. Young adults may not always be open to assistance immediately after the death of their mother. They may go on without receiving adequate assistance; however, they likely feel like they need to talk out their late-grief issues later, for example when they start dating.

They may become more childish after experiencing death in the hope of feeling more secure. On the other hand, they may distance themselves from the adults in their lives and bottle up their feelings. Young people are already going through a difficult period as they figure out who they are and how the world works.

When they are grieving, youth may withdraw from others, including adults. It is difficult to know how they are doing and what kind of help they require because of this. A physical reaction to death in young adults may be disruptive sleep, fatigue, lethargy, constant distraction, an inability to focus, change in bowel habits and appetite, and panic attacks. Grief is a difficult and complicated period of loss, but it is a natural part of life.

It is important to remember that grieving youngsters are not sick. They can cope with grief and grow from it if they understand what is going on and receive adequate support. Understanding the grief response as a process can help you figure out how to best support them. Youngsters may experience each stage differently. For example, the denial stage may be particularly strong in teens while anger is showcased as disrespectful and violent. Bargaining may take a different turn in teens, where they may opt for spiritual sources, sometimes different from what they have been raised to practice. Depression can be hard to detect in teens, but they may still fall into a pitch of despair. Teens may go back and forth through the acceptance stage just like adults do.

If we consider grief as a journey, it is the responsibility of adults to assist young people in navigating it. Young people are unlikely to want an adult with them, but they do require opportunities to reflect on their own journeys. Most importantly, they require adults who check in with them regularly to ensure they are on the right track. They must make it clear that they are also available for advice when needed.

Youth require someone who is strong and already in a close relationship with them, like the father when the mother passes away. The father in this instance may also be grieving themselves, so supporting a teenager at the same time could be a challenge. They must be given space to express their emotions with security. They should also be allowed to make decisions themselves.

As a parent, do not be afraid to enlist the help of other responsible adults to assist your child. Some young people find it easier to communicate with someone not related to them. Encourage them to speak to their school counselor about their feelings if they are overwhelmed. This is especially useful if the remaining parent is also struggling with grief.

Do not hesitate to ask for extra help at school if you notice your kid is slacking off through this difficult time, and make sure you monitor their academic performance. Try to get them back to their routine before death and encourage them to go back to former extracurricular activities.

Teenagers frequently feel compelled to make others believe that they have complete control over their lives. As a result, they may be hesitant to express feelings of sadness, hurt, or anger. This is especially true for boys, who may believe that expressing strong emotions is not cool or manly. A teen's feelings that remain bottled up can lead to depression, anxiety, and other mental health issues.

Grief is not a disease that requires curing but rather a process one learns to incorporate into their life. Essentially, helping youth with bereavement boils down to effective communication, valuing their needs, and offering caring support. This can be achieved via support groups, therapy, and specific youth programs.

Professionals helping youth through bereavement usually educate by turning the difficult time experienced through grief into an opportunity for growth. Young people are already in the process of figuring out who they are and how they fit into society. It can be tough to tell the difference between grief expressions and normal adolescent changes because of this.

It is not important to try to figure out what the difference is. The most important thing is to support the young person in their current situation. Children and teenagers who have lost a parent or sibling will require ongoing attention, reassurance, and support. It's not unusual for sadness to rear its ugly head again years later. This can happen as they progress through life's stages and grow as individuals.

If your teen is grieving, it takes patience and, in some cases, a willingness to enlist the help of others for grief and loss treatment. Be sure your son or daughter is aware that you are there and willing to assist. With your help, your teen can overcome his or her grief and move on, having developed grief-coping skills for the future.

Be ready to be questioned by your teenager about any concerns they have about life and death; although this may be a vague topic, be ready to answer their questions and discuss them. Weddings, graduations, learning to drive, birthdays, and first jobs are all milestones and rituals in their lives, and they likely imagined their loved one would be a part of them. It is common for children to be sad about upcoming rites of passage and then be sad all over again when they happen.

Chapter 12:
Gender Differences and Grief

G ender and cultural factors have an impact on how people grieve. People's emotional processing and expression are influenced by many factors. Men and women often react differently to grief, even though generalizations do not apply. However, recognizing and supporting individual differences is more important than whether a response is more common in men or women.

Many men are raised to believe that they must suppress their emotions. Crying may have been regarded as a sign of weakness among boys. People under pressure to be strong and independent may try to hide their emotions or avoid talking about them. It should come as no surprise that men and women are profoundly different in a variety of ways, one of which manifests in the area of grief. Understanding how gender differences affect how people grieve can be beneficial.

Grief in men

Men are more likely to turn inward rather than express themselves outwardly when grieving. They may be less likely to cry, express themselves verbally, or talk openly about their grief. They might completely avoid discussing the death of a loved one. Many men do not seek out conversations to help them cope with their grief. They may experience feelings of failure because of their inability to save their mother from death, for example.

Instead of expressing grief, a man would like to move on. Some men may feel compelled to make changes in their lives. Rather than using resources to grieve, they try to manage grief on their own. Men may cope with grief by participating in physically-demanding or repetitive activities. Some seek distraction or release through physical activity, manual labor, yard work, etc..

They begin to take charge of the family's needs. After a death, many feel obligated to care for family members by handling the finances, planning the funeral, or taking over the house. Working more may be motivated by the desire to improve the family's financial security, but it may also be a necessary diversion from feelings of loss and pain.

They might begin to share activities and experiences with family members. Men may have a difficult time expressing grief. They may attempt to connect with loved ones by participating in activities together. Alternatively, they might isolate themselves. Some men prefer to be left alone while they work through their grief. They may become enraged at their inability to be alone or avoid social situations for fear of losing control.

Men often express their grief physically or cognitively. They think more than they feel. They are more focused on actively responding to grief by doing. They exhibit the more masculine way of grieving. Men often say they do not know how to support their female loved ones or deal with the emotion and pain that comes with grief.

Men are more at ease with life changes, such as taking on new roles and responsibilities because of a loved one's death. Learning new non-traditional roles like cooking and cleaning helps them cope with their grief. Males frequently regard social relationships as opportunities to share activities rather than emotions. They frequently claim they already know the story in their heads and do not need to narrate it. They want to fix it, and this can depend on their resources, often suppressing their feelings and emotions.

Men claim they suppress their emotions because they do not want to show weakness. They are often respected as powerful individuals; and as a result, they may be given or accept little social support. Little boys have traditionally been taught not to cry, while little girls have been comforted. Men, overall, are inward thinkers who consider the situation rather than the emotional response. They are not less emotional or responsive to those around them because of this; they simply have a different way of looking at emotional responses.

Grief in women

Women are more susceptible than men to share their grief with others. They are more open to making connections and accepting help from others. Women are more likely to feel alone when grieving. they are more likely to feel isolated and alone, especially if other family members have difficulty communicating their feelings or do not share their ability to improve their grief.

Women try to make connections with others, believing that talking about the loss of their mother aids in the healing process. They may be irritated by others' inability to share their grief. When others are unable to join them in working through it, women may become enraged or resentful. They may deal with their grief by talking about it. They often talk about their loss with friends and family to help them process their emotions. They may be looking for help. During the grieving process, women are more likely than men to seek help from both outside and within the family.

Women experiment with forming new social networks. They may reach out to existing social networks or form new ones as they process and express their grief, particularly those who can empathize with their loss. They might also begin to question or blame others. If they are unable to share their grief and work through it together, some may question their partners or spouses because they often feel they are not on the same page. Women may turn to writing to express their grief. Reading and writing journals, stories, or books may help some feel less isolated by allowing them to interact with others.

Women are more emotional than men and might work through their grief by talking about it. They claim that telling their story over and over helps them handle and work through the grief. They confide in friends, convey their emotions and feelings externally, and feel their way through the grief. Women have expressed their dissatisfaction with men who show little emotion and refuse to discuss the person who died.

Women may interpret this as cold behavior and conclude that the man is not mourning . Traditionally, a grieving woman seeks out support. She can seek out those who can comprehend and listen to her as she expresses her feelings. She is not looking to fix anything; rather, she wants to regain her perspective and understand why she is grieving.

Grieving together

It is useful to keep in mind that grieving is necessary. Listening to others' experiences of grief may make you feel less alone and more normal on your own. Everyone wants to be recognized and accepted. One person cannot provide all the assistance that another requires. Grief after the loss of a mother is a lifelong journey with changing needs. A variety of resources are available to assist grieving family members. Reading books by authors who share a similar grief perspective can be beneficial.

In times of grief, support groups help people connect and feel a sense of belonging. Professional assistance is also available. Marriage and family counseling can be a valuable tool for helping family members accept their grieving discrepancies and find ways to grieve around each other. This message is changing, so hopefully, education will spread. These conflicting gender messages can last a person's entire life and create confusion between grieving males and females. For both genders, this can lead to frustration, anger, and a sense of isolation in their grief.

In times of grief, both men and women require assistance. They need to hear from others that their emotions are normal, as are their reactions, and they can live and love again. It is critical to emphasize that whether you are a man or a woman grieving the loss of a loved one, if you refuse to express your grief in any form, you will likely face serious consequences later in life. For those who have lost someone and are willing to express their grief fully, in whatever way they are comfortable doing it, it is a make-or-break decision.

You can set yourself up for a lifetime of ailments, bitterness, anger, and a lack of connection to life if you do not express your grief. When it comes to gender differences, it is important to remember that neither approach is correct nor incorrect; they are just different. Both sexes can benefit from each other's experiences. People can learn to support one another without trying to change them if they learn to understand and accept their differences. Grief is a very personal and individual experience, and everyone goes through it in their unique way. It is hoped that those who are embarking on this journey will find comforting support along the way.

There is no such thing as a standard or traditional grief response. It is normal to experience a wide range of emotions and behaviors. Some responses can be gender-specific while others, however, may not. The most important thing is that each person feel accepted and supported by other family members in their grief. Everyone, regardless of how they are grieving, requires support.

After losing a mother, people need to be reassured that their reactions are normal. Everyone tries to cope in their unique way. Families, on the other hand, must find ways to connect and come together amid their grief.

Chapter 13:
The Physical Impact of Grief

I t is phenomenal how physically painful grief can be. The pain in your heart is palpable. A memory triggers your stomach to clench or sends shivers down your spine. Your mind races, and your heart races with it. Your body electrifies with energy to the point where you can barely sleep some nights. You are so tired some nights that you fall asleep immediately. You wake up the next day exhausted and spend most of the day in bed.

Several studies have revealed the powerful effects of grief on the body. Grief increases inflammation, which can exacerbate existing health problems and create new ones, such as ulcerative colitis, among others. It wreaks havoc on the immune system, leaving you vulnerable to infection. Grief's heartbreak can raise blood pressure and increase the risk of blood clots. Intense grief can wreak havoc on the heart muscle, resulting in "broken heart syndrome," a type of heart disease with real symptoms like a heart attack. The emotional and physical aspects of grief are linked to stress.

Physical and emotional stress are processed by the same systems in the body; emotional stress can activate the nervous system just as easily as physical threats. Chronic medical problems can be exacerbated by elevated adrenaline and blood pressure when stress becomes constant. Emotional pain activates the same brain regions as physical pain, according to research. This could explain why painkillers like opioids have been shown to help with emotional pain.

When grief becomes a prolonged phase, depression is a complication, not a normal part of the grieving process. Depression increases the risk of grief-related health complications and frequently necessitates treatment, so knowing how to recognize its symptoms is crucial. Certain emotional patterns can distinguish between normal grief and depression.

Unlike the more persistent low mood and agony of major depressive disorder, sad thoughts and feelings in normal grief come in waves or bursts, followed by periods of respite. Depressed people experience guilt and worthlessness, as well as a limited ability to experience or anticipate any pleasure or joy.

Complicated grief is a type of long-term, prevalent grief that does not improve on its own. It occurs when some of the natural thoughts, feelings, or behaviors that accompany acute grief take root and obstruct the ability to accept the reality of the loss. Attempts to ignore the grief and deny or rewrite what happened are common symptoms.

Complicated grief raises the risk of physical and mental health issues such as depression, anxiety, insomnia, suicidal thoughts and behaviors, as well as medical problems. Contemplation, or repetitive, negative, self-focused thought, is a way to avoid problems, according to research. Ruminators divert their attention away from painful truths by concentrating on negative material that is less threatening than the truths they wish to avoid.

This way of thinking has a strong connection to depression. Rumination and avoidance consume energy and obstruct the body's and mind's natural abilities to integrate new realities and heal. Attempts to avoid facing the reality of loss can lead to fatigue, weakened immunity, increased inflammation, and the prolongation of other illnesses.

When a loved one passes, your social role shifts as well. This can have an impact on your sense of self and meaning. Caregivers face particularly difficult role transitions. Even before a loved one dies, the physical and emotional demands of caregiving can deplete them such that losing the person they cared for can leave them feeling purposeless.

According to research, caregivers not only experience high levels of stress during periods of intense caregiving, but they also lack the time and energy to care for their own health. When the care beneficiary passes away, this can result in the emergence of new or resurfacing of previously inactive health problems. During and after a loss, the stress of adjusting to changes in life and health can increase vulnerability and deplete adaptive reserves for coping with bereavement. Self-care, both emotional and physical, is critical for easing grief's complications and accelerating recovery. Physical and mental health can be improved by exercising, spending time in nature, getting enough sleep, and talking to loved ones.

Most of the time, normal grief does not necessitate professional help. Grief is a rational, instinctive reaction to loss. Adaptation happens naturally as does healing, especially with time and the support of loved ones and friends. Social support, self-acceptance, and good self-care, according to grief researchers, are usually helpful in getting people through normal grief. However, these researchers believe that to recover from complicated grief and depression, people require professional assistance.

Grief may manifest in a variety of physical symptoms apart from emotional ones. You may experience fatigue, nausea, decreased immunity, changes in weight, aches, pain, and sleep disturbances. If these symptoms persist, it is important to seek medical assistance. The physical impacts of grief are very natural because of the deep connection with the mother. You experience such symptoms because someone available to you is no longer there.

One would not grieve because one's life vanished from the world, but because that one life is significant to them. The closer you were with your mother, the bigger the physical impact is going to be. Bonding does not only depend on psychological aspects, but also on physical aspects. Therefore, the body grieves in its own way. A lot of yogis in the Hindu religion believe physical impact during grief mostly occurs if you experience the death of a loved one up to twenty-one years of age. If you're a senior man, you may experience physical pain following grief, but this is minimal. If you are an older woman who suddenly lost her mother, your grief is going to be mostly emotional and psychological. You may still experience physical pain, but it is very unlikely.

If one is emotionally stable and psychologically in control, they can handle grief, especially if they are not struggling with physical pain on top of everything else caused by grief. The physical pain experienced by the body following the death of a loved one is dependent on the connections between the two bodies.

The death of a mother can be more devastating for the mind and cause emotional and psychological turmoil. In comparison, if a wife loses her husband, she is more likely to experience physical pain because the physical connection she had with the deceased is different and can will be lacking after he is gone.

Once the physical suffering is taken care, the individual can better deal with the psychological and emotional issues caused because of the loss; therefore seeking medical assistance for such symptoms is very important, as stated above.

Chapter 14:
How to Deal with Regrets

Regret encompasses a wide range of negative feelings, including self-blame, sorrow, anger, and a sense of personal responsibility for not acting differently. Living in a state of regret can lower your quality of life and make you unhappy. While regrets are difficult to bear, you can learn to let them go and move on with your life.

If you find yourself feeling sad, depressed, and bad about yourself because of regret, it might be time to let it go. Accepting that you made a mistake or wishing things had gone differently might be necessary. Rather than putting yourself down, you must accept and forgive yourself at some point. Write a letter to the deceased person if you are having trouble letting go of your regret. Mention the positive aspects of the relationship as well as what you wish you would have said or done.

Place this letter in a special location or store it in a special place. Recognize that a variety of factors may have contributed to this regret. Given the circumstances, you may have been under a lot of stress, had financial difficulties, relied on faulty information, or been in a situation where your decision-making abilities were impaired. Exempt yourself of any unjustified blame. Speak to someone who is not cynical to get a better viewpoint from someone who is not biased. You can talk to someone not involved in the situation, such as a friend or therapist.

Even though the outcome was not what you had hoped for, you did what you thought was best at the time so release yourself from all responsibility. You can become a captive of your own negative feelings if enslaved by resentment. Accept the fact that you can still make mistakes and have lapses in judgment. It is not worth being miserable every day about something you cannot change. Instead, learn to forgive yourself and make better decisions in the future. You have suffered because of your decisions, but you are now willing to forgive yourself and move on from there. Allow yourself to grow because of this experience.

Regret is a feeling with origins in the past. It is difficult to live in the past when your life is taking place right now. Focusing on the present moment entails letting go of previous experiences, thoughts, or behavioral patterns. Bring your thoughts and awareness into the present moment and tune in more to the present. Sit quietly and concentrate on what is going on right now. You can train yourself to focus on something more productive than regretful feelings with practice. Make paying attention to your breathing a routine.

Concentrate on your breathing, paying attention to your inhales and exhales. Turn to your senses if you are feeling overwhelmed by regret-related negative feelings and cannot seem to break the cycle. Meditation can be a helpful tool here. If you are drowning in regret, you are probably not living in the present. Concentrate on just one sense at a time. Begin with your senses and see what you discover. Slowly engage each sense one by one and return to the present moment. You have the ability to return and distance yourself from regret by focusing on your senses.

Stop passing judgment and making assessments of yourself and your actions. Instead of categorizing yourself as good or bad, learn to accept yourself as you are. Accept that you are constantly learning and evolving, and each day brings you closer to becoming a kinder, better version of you. Kindness, mindfulness, and connection with others can help you practice self-compassion.

When you look back on what you said or did while your mother was alive, the grieving process becomes even more painful. There is no way to apologize or make amends. You cannot go back in time and change your behavior. It is natural to have regrets about things you said and did while your mother was alive. You are not by yourself, you are not a bad person, and you do not have to despise yourself.

Practice taking care of and thinking about yourself. Treat yourself as if you were your own best friend. You should be concerned with your thoughts, feelings, actions, and reactions. When you feel unworthy, ask "What would I say to a friend who is feeling this way?" If your regret is for someone who has passed but involves living people, sort out the unspoken apologies. If you can act on something, even if ashamed, do so.

It is preferable to say what must be said rather than to live in regret. If your mother dies and there were issues with other family members, resolve them while they are still here. While regret may appear to be entirely negative, it can also have positive aspects.

Regret can help you reconsider your choices and how you want to live in the future. Then you must decide: do you want to keep living this way or do you want to make a change? You have experience with regret already at this point, so you would avoid doing it again. Regret may cause you to reflect on how you treat others in your life. If your mother died, you might regret not paying her enough attention or making time for her.

This can lead to a new perspective on relationships, with you prioritizing people in your life in ways you have never done before. Recognize that life is a journey with many paths that intersect along the way. Rather than feeling bad about yourself or that you have made mistakes, recognize that you have had opportunities to learn and grow. Recognize that growth is happening now, even if it did not happen in the past. Recognize the time you did spend with someone before they died. Consider the positive aspects of the relationship, including what you value and what the other person used to value.

You can't change what has already happened, but you can be grateful for the memories you created together. Remind yourself of the positive aspects of your relationship with your mother. Even if the person has passed away, gratitude allows you to appreciate and celebrate the person's impact in the present moment. Consider the positive aspects of the relationship in both your and this person's lives. Thank each other for the part you played in each other's lives. Gratitude has numerous long-term physical, emotional, and social advantages. Because it is impossible to be grateful and upset at the same time, gratitude can help block negative emotions.

Your regrets will fester and grow if you keep them hidden. Talking about the things you regret saying and doing cannot make the pain of losing someone you care about go away, but it can help you start the healing process. By bringing your statements and deeds into the open, you can begin to deal with the regrets that have been tormenting you. Grief is not remedied by time alone.

When someone you care about dies, letting time pass is not the best way to deal with regret. If you keep looking away from the guilt, shame and regret you are experiencing, it cannot go away. Regret follows you around. You made errors, allowed yourself to be consumed by negative or toxic emotions, and made self-centered decisions. You were truly doing the best you could at the time, even if you now believe you could have done better. Regret may appear, but there is nothing you can do about it right now. You cannot drive it away; it, like pain, eventually finds you.

Chapter 15:
How Losing Your Mother Impacts Your brain

No matter how old you are, the trauma of losing a parent has a profound effect on everyone. The anguish is so great that studies have shown that the death of your mother can alter your brain chemistry with long-term physical consequences.

Grief affects your brain in a profound and complicated way. According to research, the posterior cingulate cortex, frontal cortex, and cerebellum, which process grief, are also the same regions of the brain that retrieve memories and dwell on the past. They are also the same parts that control our sleep and hunger. This explains why many people experience an increase in sleep or the reverse, insomnia, at times, or significant changes in appetite when in a deep state of grief or depression.

The death of a parent, whether expected or unexpected, brings with it a range of emotions. When a child loses a parent at a young age, it is usually a sudden loss, which can cause younger children and adults to go through long periods of denial and anger. When a death is expected, having time to prepare for and accept the loss allows you to say goodbye and find a good support system. This could explain why other studies show that the loss of a parent has a greater impact on younger adults.

Losing a parent can increase the chances of developing long-term emotional and mental health problems such as depression, anxiety, and substance abuse. Many have complicated relationships with their parents, and some do not even have one at all. Unresolved emotions like anger and resentment have a long-term impact on mental health. When a parent passes, there is no way to reconcile or have your feelings validated.

When it comes to a parent's death, there is no such thing as getting over it. While your brain is adjusting to the loss, you might feel lost and sad. This loss functions as a stressor and triggers the pituitary gland located in the brain to release adrenocorticotrophin (ACTH). ACTH stimulates the adrenal glands to release a stress hormone called cortisol. This hormone is released in times of temporary stressors, but grief is a persistent stressor, so your body becomes overloaded with this hormone for a long time. This weakens your immune system, causing fatigue and malaise. Although some losses may be expected, these effects still occur in the body. During grief, some parts of the brain are overactive and may lead to despair and stress. The anterior cingulate cortex is the part of the brain that controls emotions. This area may struggle with controlling irritants, causing the heart rate to increase because of its inability to control emotions at this time.

During depression, as part of grief, the brain is also affected. The amygdala, the part of the brain used to regulate sleep patterns and mood, can be affected. The hippocampus is another area of the brain affected by grief and depression that is used to regulate memory and stress hormones. The whole process of grief and depression can affect your body by causing your organs to malfunction or shut off at times.

You may find yourself sleeping more or less than you are used to. Your brain may feel foggy, and you may find it hard to remember things. These feelings and reactions are normal and can slowly start changing into a better and brighter mood. To move from sadness, anger, and depression to acceptance can take up to a year. Therapy whether group or individual, and cognitive behavioral treatment also facilitate this process. Physical exercise increases concentration and memory. Bringing back memories of your loved ones releases neurons in the brain's reward system. This helps you cherish memories with the deceased and provides the capability of acknowledging that although they are gone, their memory always remains.

Regardless of the kind of relationship you had or what kind of parent they were, your mother was always there for you. This has a profound and permanent mental, physical, and emotional impact on you for the rest of your life.

Chapter 16:
Coping with Your Mother's Reappearance

Y ou may feel like your mom has passed, but she still shows up in material things. This may be more common when you are struggling with hard times, like when you are nervous, or things are more emotionally challenging. It could be a song on the radio that feels like she is speaking directly to you or the kindness and compassion of a stranger in a store. She eventually reappears, and you sense her presence and love.

If you find yourself in a difficult situation, your mother's reappearance may not take your anxiety away, but it can give you hope. It feels like a hug sent from heaven. It may surround you with love and faith, just what you need during trying times. Your late mother may appear in spirit. She is present in those moments when you require and yearn for her. She is always there when you need her. All you must do now is remember this.

It is critical to pay close attention. Remind yourself that she can still be with you in difficult moments, albeit in a spiritual form - a different kind of role with a new perspective. She is a mother, after all. Even after they have passed away, mothers keep their promises.

She never missed a special occasion or an opportunity to be with her children. Mothers are with you in those moments when you need them. Look around and pay attention because they are with you if you take a spiritual or religious approach. This happens mostly after you have experienced grief for a while and are transitioning to accepting the loss and learning to live with it.

Initially, your mother's reappearance in material things acts as a constant reminder. Her belongings surround you. There is a reminder everywhere you look, from her toothbrush in the bathroom to the dirty clothes in the washing basket, from their books on the dresser to the keys by the door. While some of these items may be comforting, many are simply small and painful reminders of her absence. If that is the case, you will have to look for a way to clear these reminders to help you go through the grief process in a less challenging manner.

However, the thought of seeing these items in the trash may be the only thing more painful than seeing them every day. Find someone who can dispose of those half-empty plastic containers, to-do lists, and medicines if you cannot. Friends and extended family members are frequently eager to assist but lack the necessary skills. Consider this one way you can assist them in assisting you. Tell them what you want to get rid of and ask them to dispose of it and take the trash with them when they leave so you do not have to.

Consider the everyday reminders that are especially distressing for you while your friend is there. These could be items you do not want to give or throw away but find difficult to see every day. Put them in a box or a room you do not use very often. These items can be anything from Mom's favorite mug to her blanket. Place them out of the way until you are ready to begin facing these significant items every day. You can eventually learn to cherish these items and no longer view them as hurtful reminders.

Chapter 17:
Adjusting to the New Norm

There is no doubt that some days are more painful than others when you are mourning. Many individuals are unaware that depression is cyclical. You may feel better for a short time before returning to the depths of depression. Just when you believe you have gotten over it, another surge of grief hits you, and you experience what seems to be a crushing loss.

People with good intentions want to hasten your grieving process. They will do their best to keep you occupied, and some may avoid mentioning your mother's name out of fear of hurting you. You must, however, allow yourself to grieve. It will catch up to you if you try to keep busy and put it out of your mind. You're going to feel it at some point.

It is best to let things happen as they will. Certain days are more important than others, and they remind everyone about the individual who died more directly. These can be particularly challenging. Sundays are frequently connected with family gatherings, anniversaries, as are holidays such as Christmas and other occasions. They are all days when the absence of a loved one is felt. A person's birthday, for example, can be a difficult time when you recall special parties and the presents you gave them. After someone's burial, a birthday is normally not a joyful day.

Other occasions like your birthday, weddings, and Mother's Day can also be hard to deal with. These can be challenging because they remind us of happier times when the individual was there. It can be discouraging for those who do not grasp the process when you do not appear to be doing better or it seems like you are getting worse rather than stronger.

Still, as I am sure you are aware, sadness comes and goes. Grief attacks is a term used to describe these episodes. There are many reasons, several of which are commonplace: sitting in a popular restaurant with your loved one, smelling a certain perfume, or hearing a particular song on the radio. There are so many moments that remind you of the person who has passed, and each has the power to make you miss them all over again.

These special occasions can be very difficult to overcome. It is important not to think of them as setbacks, because as difficult as they are, they are simply an opportunity to come to terms with your loss a bit more completely. Grief encourages people to recall rather than forget. Ignoring the occasion or pretending that it is just another day is unnatural because it just adds to the uneasiness of the situation.

Avoiding the problem needs more resources than confronting it. Observe these holidays and special events in the method most convenient for you. If you would like to make some modifications, go ahead and do so. It's important to remember that there's no right and wrong way to handle these scenarios. If you've decided how, you can keep track of time and what you are able to do easily, and then inform your family and friends.

Allow yourself to experience and express your emotions. Those special days can amplify feelings of bereavement. Share your worries, fears, and emotions with a friend or support network. Recognize that during the holidays, the need for assistance is often stronger. Try to get enough sleep since these events can be mentally and physically exhausting. Recognize the role of your loved one in the household. To quietly include your loved one, consider lighting a memorial candle at the dinner table or in the home. If it is not too painful, listen to music that the deceased enjoyed or look at photos or recordings.

Do not hold back from having an awesome time. Of course, it is normal to feel depressed, but it does not have to be all bad. Laughter and joy are not considered impolite. Allow you and your family members to enjoy and celebrate one another. You and your family and friends can get together and exchange special memories or hear stories about your mother. Recalling amusing events can have a special calming effect.

True, your precious one died, but they still lived so make their birthday a life-affirming event. Make their wedding or any celebration a day to be grateful for what you had and to mourn what you have missed. Even though their absence is great, take time on that day to consider and be grateful for the deceased. Try to recall the pleasant times you had with your mother. A birthday is, after all, a celebration of life.

So, what do you do to honor her life while still remembering her death? Make the best of the time you have. Initially, you may pay a visit to the cemetery as you are in the early stages of grief; but as time passes you can learn to deal with these special occasions and use them to honor her past presence and remember the memories you had together.

Be constructive rather than reactive. To put it another way, do anything to regain control of the day. Consider it an additional chance to grieve, miss your mother, and peel back another layer of sorrow. It is unnatural to behave as if nothing has happened. Make an effort to remember and grieve. Pair the grief over their loss with joy over their survival, and these tough days can be more important.

Of course, you are upset that someone you care about is not there, and that is understandable. You should be appreciative for what you had yet still grieve what you have lost. Do not let reminiscing distract you from what you have now. You miss the person who cannot be here, but there are kids, family, and friends with whom you can spend the day. It cannot make the sadness go anywhere, but it can make it a lot better. The people around you are your support system and have been probably since the death of your mother. Celebrate them and appreciate their presence through this hard time.

When it comes to grieving at tough moments such as special holidays, you have two options. Will you rule the day, or do you want the day to control you? You can either let sorrow rule you, or you can learn to control it. Accepting your sorrow can make a big difference, so acknowledge that your mother is no longer but you are still enjoying her presence.

Remember that you have the choice of crying because she has passed away or smiling because she existed. Alternatively, you should be able to do it at the same time. Be ready for tough days, expect and embrace them, and do all you can to create a memorable day.

Chapter 18:
Finding Grief-coping Techniques

Y ou were born to your mother. Throughout your childhood, she fed and cared for you. In most cases, the mother is the one who has the most responsibility for child care and is at home with the children more often than the father. When you break up with your first boyfriend or girlfriend, when you need advice or have a problem, you go to your mother. Your mother is not only your most enthusiastic follower, but she is also a part of you.

She could be both your mother and your best friend. It is as if you have lost a piece of yourself. No one is ever as interested in what you do or as proud of you as your mother. Mothers are often the ones who hold families together. They are the ones who communicate with all the family members and disseminate information. They plan get-togethers, keep the family home in order, and are the center of family life. When the mother passes away, the family either disintegrates or you must assume her role as the primary communicator and organizer. Even if you did not have the best relationship, her death can be traumatic. You do not have any more chances to make things right. Although the death of a parent is an inevitable part of growing up and affects everyone, it is still devastating. However, many people are taken aback by how much it affects them. Their friends and family may not realize how devastating it is, especially if they have been old or ill for a long time, and the death was anticipated.

You cannot hack your way out of grief. There is nothing that can put a broken heart back together. However, you may discover that grieving can enrich your life in surprising ways. Although this sounds absurd now, there are things that grief can teach you to help you cope through this time. Here are some mechanisms one can adopt to help cope after the death of a mother:

They lived before they died. You may drift away from your siblings and loved ones after losing your mother, and by the time you rekindle relationships and get closer to your family members because you want to retain those relationships, they will help you through the later stages of grief.

No one can replace your mother. Although it feels fatal in the beginning to have such a void after death, you can learn to live with it and never expect it to be replaced by anyone else. You will come to appreciate the female role models in your life. You can learn to let that guilt feeling go and make room for others in your life. Despite the holes you carry, healing is an act of expansion, not substitution.

Take it easy on yourself. You may be berating yourself for things you could not control as part of your grieving process, and your brain fog may feel like yet another failure. But the fog dissipates over time, and your memories return. This can be interpreted as your mind going into survival mode, complete with its own set of coping mechanisms. It is possible that being kind to yourself has never been your strong suit, and grief likes to make guilt its companion. Meditation, yoga, and journal writing are three techniques that can help you remember that being kind is more powerful than listening to your inner critic.

Make use of whatever works for you. There is no one-size-fits-all approach to grieving, and I can't stress that enough. It is a lot of bouncing around until you find something that works. Death, like healing, is unpredictably unpredictable. You may not be a religious person but find comfort in a group run by a priest. You may never have read a self-help book if it was not for your mother's death, but one has helped you. You may not be enrolled in a sports team but playing football or basketball as you used to when little can help you distract yourself from grief and seek freedom from that guilt feeling.

Although grieving is a difficult process, it does not necessitate punishing yourself for what has occurred. You must find activities that allow you to relax and divert your attention from your grief. Participate in activities that make you happy and laugh. Laughter can help you unwind. Even if having fun is the last thing on your mind, engage in activities during this difficult time.

Resilience triumphs. Self-pity and gratitude are two sides of the same coin: the latter will benefit you, while the former will provide you with nothing. If you lost your mom at twenty years old, you may feel like twenty years is too little and everyone wishes for endless time with their mother; but you look at the glass half full and be grateful for the beautiful memories you have lived together.

Choose to succeed. One of grief's many tricks: it makes you believe you do not deserve to be happy. It is much easier to self-destruct than to care for oneself. Everyone has their own constructive coping mechanisms, and it is worth it in the long run to choose them, even if difficult. You will not be watered like a plant; you must choose to succeed.

Things will get better, but it does so on its schedule. Grief time is different from regular time. There are always good days and bad days. This is the agreement that everyone makes when they become a human. Once the worst days are over, you develop a greater appreciation for the little things found in everyday life. Healing takes time, but only if you are willing to put in the effort to grieve.

Allow your losses to draw attention to your gains. This can be hard to comprehend, especially soon after the loss. You may not recognize it at first, but it may be that because of the loss, you started writing. Because your mother has passed, you managed to move away from your hometown and start a new life somewhere you always wanted to be. You may have chosen to dive into a new course or finally graduate, something you have been putting off for a long time. You may have opted for this as a distraction, but you managed and have succeeded.

Progress is marked by heartbreak. Grief strengthens us so that we can cope with the inevitable losses in our lives. This is not a negative viewpoint. This is the belief that the benefits of love always outweigh the risks.

We become novices because of our grief. Death is the only universal process that turns everyone into beginners. Grief, on the other hand, affects us all in different ways. There is no manual on how to deal with it. There is only so much time to figure out what works and what does not, day by day, and sometimes minute by minute. Loss can enrich your life in a variety of ways, some of which are difficult, unexpected, and even beautiful.

Do not bury your grief or your memories. Your relationship with your mother was most likely the most important one in your life. The strong emotions that her death has evoked are natural and nothing to be afraid of. People often avoid strong emotions because they are afraid of becoming trapped in them. Do not run from your grief, but do not wear it like a suffocating blanket either. Your capacity to grieve demonstrates your ability to love. Share your emotions with the people who matter to you, such as your spouse, friends, and family. Your siblings can empathize with your feelings about your mother the most.

Do not subject yourself to pain by exposing yourself to triggers. To put it another way, stay away from people who are sure to cause you grief. Looking over the greeting card shelves at all the Mother's Day cards, scrolling through Facebook or Instagram and looking at all the pictures of loving parents, and going to restaurants during the peak of Mother's Day family gatherings are just a few examples.

Make specific plans for the day. This can be very beneficial for days like Mother's Day or her birthday. You are less likely to feel sad and overwhelmed if you have a plan for how your day will go. Self-compassion and acceptance are the best things you can do for yourself. If you must spend time alone, focus on self-care rather than binging on junk food and watching depressing movies. Rather, nourish your body and soul by eating well and getting some exercise. Listen to some meditation tapes, concentrate on your work, or look at some old photos or videos that bring back fond memories.

If you've been dreading starting this book, now is the time. The point is to do what makes you happy, not activities that will make your loss worse. You could go for a hike or do something that will nourish your soul. If you decide you do not want to be alone, have a fallback option. Make plans with a friend or family member ahead of time who will be happy to receive your call or visit.

Planning may need to be done for every day rather than just for special occasions. After a loss, your day-to-day activities can feel different, and they might continue to change over time. It is business as usual for some people; they get up, go to work, and repeat. Others start small, such as making the bed and remembering to eat breakfast every morning. It does not matter what your routine looks like; all that matters is that you have one. Make a to-do list right away, set smaller goals, and take each day as it comes. You will feel more fulfilled and positive about yourself if you achieve these goals.

Do things that honor her: Taking a step outside of yourself to help others in need is a lovely way to honor your mother while also making you feel better. Another good idea, especially for the first Mother's Day without her, is to get together with your family. Keep the stories you tell humorous or happy!

Make your customs. The tradition for the second Sunday in May while your mother was alive was most likely to spend time with her. Now that she is gone, you can start new customs to make the day even more memorable. You could organize an annual gathering of friends who have lost their mothers. Give these days a positive meaning. While there are no quick fixes for grieving the loss of a mother, there are ways to make the day so publicly devoted to happy families showering love on their mothers something that brings you satisfaction and community, if not happiness. This may apply to not just Mother's Day, but also to her birthday.

Understand grief and how it works. The most common emotion associated with loss is, of course, deep sadness. However, you may have a variety of other emotions during the grieving process. Depressed, angry, fearful, anxious, fatigued, empty, secluded, or in a state of delusion, shock, or disbelief are all possible emotions. You might even experience a sense of relief followed by guilt. These emotions can strike at any time, erupt without warning, and persist for as long as they are supposed to. They can also become overwhelming, interrupting your sleep, energy, desire to eat, and concentration, as well as affecting your overall health.

Although you may have come across the different stages of grief, it is important to understand that there is no linear process, and everyone can experience it in different ways. Understanding how it works, however, can be very beneficial for you during this time. It can make you aware of your feelings and emotions and help you attribute the way you are feeling to what you are experiencing. Recognize the loss. Make room for your emotions. Recognize that grief is a lifelong experience. Know that life can still be enjoyable after a loss. You can feel better with time and effort. Experts offer advice on how to cope with grief so you can eventually come to terms with it.

Be honest about your emotions. It is critical to find people with whom you feel comfortable sharing your feelings. This can include family members, close friends, work colleagues, or people who have suffered a similar loss, such as a support group. Do not try to deal with grief on your own. This is the time to lean on your family and friends the most. Tell people how you are feeling and if you are having trouble. Share your memories and experiences with others. Share your tears, your rage, and your laughter. It can help a lot with process management.

Participate in traditions. Participating in funerals or memorials can be beneficial if you have lost a loved one, no matter how difficult it may seem because it allows you to be around others who are grieving the same person you are. Doing something on your own to honor someone's memory, such as making a memory book to look back on, journaling, or participating in that person's favorite activity can be a source of comfort. Birthdays, anniversaries, and other occasions that provide an opportunity to reflect are highly beneficial. Simply lighting a candle on their birthday can bring back happier memories and ignite discussion, helping you feel less alone.

Rewire your brain. Triggers correlate with grief. They can be as insignificant as a particular scent or as monumental as a significant life event. Simply feeling the emotions, taking careful note of them, and then adjusting is one way to deal with them. It can be distressing to be crying years later but take a step back and consider that this person was such an important part of your life that you still have strong emotion. This is a beautiful thing that highlights the importance of your relationship.

Concentrate on your most important principles. Regularly checking in with yourself about what you are getting out of life and doing to reach your goals while staying on course and constantly focusing on pushing ahead is a healthy way to keep on track. It truly assists people in directing their lives in a meaningful and joyful manner, rather than allowing feelings of emptiness to disrupt them.

Every day, try to do one thing that supports one of your values. If knowledge is important to you, for example, read a new book on a subject you have always wanted to learn more about. Spend time each week cooking a delicious meal if nourishing your body and mind is important to feel satisfied.

Do not be afraid to ask for help. There's no one-size-fits-all way to know when it's time to seek help; but if you need it, don't be ashamed to try a professional therapist or even a trusted mentor, like a pastor or coach. However, when grief feels constant, as if there is no way to turn off your pain, it can quickly escalate into full-fledged depression.

Push yourself to socialize. When you are sad or depressed, it is important to keep your social life active. It helps you relax by steering you away from the source of your stress. Similarly, when you socialize and converse with others, you can express all your bottled-up emotions. Socialization could initially appear to be extremely intimidating, but with practice, you will reap the benefits. Your circle must be a positive one, now more than ever. Positive things help you cope with grief much more effectively. Being surrounded by people and the things you enjoy lifts your spirits and brings a smile to your face. If you enjoy music, for example, getting together with a few friends and listening to your favorite songs is a great idea. Painting, pottery, gardening, and baking are all enjoyable activities to do alone or with friends.

Engage in physical activity. When grieving, the last thing you want to do is exercise. When you're feeling under the weather and depressed, you will be surprised at how beneficial exercise can be. Activity aids in the development of energy and the reduction of fatigue. You may notice an improvement in your mood, making it easier to cope with grief. There is no need to do exercises that are extremely difficult or strenuous. Keep the sessions brief and enjoyable. Ensure to look after yourself during this trying time in your life. Rather than spending the entire day in bed or locked inside your room, get enough sleep to rest properly, eat healthy foods, and engage in activities that relax your mind.

Be lenient with yourself. You're mourning the loss of a loved one. You are going through a difficult period. Some days will be brighter than others, and many will be quite dark. It is critical to understand your limitations and do not overdo things that cause you harm. Allow yourself to relax and let go of your usual routine. People recognize that you are not in the best mental state to fulfill commitments, and that is just fine. You will deal with external pressure better.

Various things provide comfort to different people. Taking a walk benefits some individuals: others find that a long, hot bath is sufficient. It is not so much what you do as it is about do something for yourself. There may be tunes, fragrances, or images that provide comfort. It is the sight of a hummingbird for me. Figure out what works best for you. Do not allow anyone take these moments away from you. Now that you have the tools to help overcome grief, you can use some of the methods mentioned above to make this difficult process a little easier.

Chapter 19:
How to be a Support system for Someone who has Lost their Mother

It is difficult to know what to say or do when someone you care about is grieving a loss. Many intense and painful emotions, such as depression, anger, guilt, and deep sadness, plague the bereaved. They often feel isolated and alone in their grief; the intense pain and difficult emotions make people hesitant to help. You might be worried about invading their privacy, saying the wrong thing, or making your loved one feel even worse during this difficult time.

Perhaps you believe there is little you can do to improve things. That is completely understandable. But do not let your discomfort keep you from reaching out to a grieving person.

The bereaved needs your help now more than ever before. You don't have to know everything, offer any piece of expert advice, or say and do everything perfectly. The most important thing you can do for a mourning person is just to be there for them. Your presence and care can help your loved one cope with the pain and continue to recover steadily.

To be a support system to someone grieving, you must understand what they are going through. Make sure you familiarize yourself with the process and understand that although there may be a set of steps involved, there is no fixed schedule. You will be better equipped to assist a bereaved friend or family member if you have a better understanding of grief and how it is healed.

Grief does not always progress in a predictable and orderly manner. It can be a thrilling ride, with unforeseen highs, lows, and downfalls. Everyone grieves in their way, so do not tell your loved one how they should feel or act. Understand and acknowledge the emotions involved in grief and how to identify them. Make sure to be available for your loved ones and reassure them that whatever is going on in their head or whatever they are feeling is perfectly normal.

While all of us are concerned with what to say to a grieving person, listening is much more critical. When the deceased person is mentioned, many well-intentioned people avoid speaking about it or change the topic. They try to avoid the grieving person altogether, knowing that nothing they say can make it better. The bereaved, on the other hand, needs assurance that their grief acknowledged, is not too painful to discuss, and their loved one cannot be forgotten. They may want to cry on your shoulder one day, and then express emotions, sit in silence, or share memories the next. You can learn from the grieving person by being present and listening compassionately. While you should never compel someone to open up, let your grieving friend or loved one know that you are willing to listen if they want to chat about their loss.

You can acknowledge the situation by letting them know you are aware of the loss. You can also express concern by saying you feel sorry about the passing away of their beloved mother. People who are grieving may find themselves repeating the same story over and over, sometimes in minute detail. Patience is required. It is a way of processing and accepting the death. The pain lessens with each retelling.

You are assisting your loved one's healing by listening patiently and compassionately. You can ask how they are feeling that day and can acknowledge their emotions so they can feel valued. Accept the way they are feeling and if you have experienced something similar, avoid comparing yourself to them. This can be harmful because no two people are the same. Do not try to make up for their loss; offering simplistic solutions or unsolicited advice can be all they need now. It is far better to simply listen to your loved one or admit you do not know what to do.

If the grieving person refuses to speak, do not push. Comfort often comes from simply being in your presence. If you are at a loss for words, simply make eye contact, squeeze their hand, or give them a warm hug. Many people who are mourning find it awkward to ask for support. They may feel guilty about being the center of attention, fear being a burden to others, or simply are too depressed to reach out.

When a person is grieving, they may not have the energy or motivation to call for help. You can offer help with the most basic of things, like clearing up the house or bringing food. Try to be consistent with your generous offers. The grieving person understands that you will be there for as long as it takes and can count on your attention without having to make the extra effort of asking repeatedly. You may offer to look after their pets, accompany them to grief group meetings, babysit their children, or simply go with them for walks in the park. Make your support is ongoing; and although they may seem fine on the outside, they may still be struggling long after the death of their mother. Keep in mind that life will never be the same again. You never get over losing a mother. The bereaved may come to terms with their loss and accept it eventually. The pain may lessen over time, but the sadness will never go away completely.

Your constant support will be golden at times. There may be days where extra support is required, such as the Christmas holiday or birthdays. A grieving person may feel depressed, confused, isolated from others, or as if they are going insane. On the other hand, if the bereaved person's symptoms do not fade or lessen over time, it is time to seek medical help. It could be a sign that normal grief has progressed into a more serious problem, such as clinical depression.

If you notice these signs, encourage the grief stricken person to seek help. Take advantage of the opportunity to do something nice in honor of a deceased member of your friend's family. Take them out to dinner! Pick up the phone or send your friend a thoughtful card to let them know you are thinking of them on this tough day.

It is natural to want to cheer up your friend. However, it is sometimes necessary to experience full grief. Although your friend may prefer to be alone, it is the thought that counts. So, invite them over to hang out; although they might refuse if they do not feel like socializing that day, they know you are there.

Encourage your friend to do more for themselves, even if it is only for a few minutes to find a way out of their grief. Take them to a beauty salon for some self-care rituals or encourage them to attend a yoga class with you. Before suggesting activities for the two of you to do together, it is a good idea to ask your friend how they want to spend the day. Then do everything you can to support the initiative. Perhaps your friend would like to pay a visit to their parents' gravesite.

Having friends and relatives who are happy to be there in the sad and painful times without attempting to remedy them - while not showing fear, discomfort, or judgment - is invaluable and something that people frequently express gratitude for. Understanding that grief is in many ways an eternal thing is an important part of being a supportive family member or friend. Your loved one may require your support not only in the immediate aftermath of their loss but also in the years ahead.

Anniversaries, holidays, birthdays, Mother's Day and weddings, and graduations can all fall somewhere on the sad to bittersweet spectrum. People frequently require practical assistance following the death of their mother for two reasons: the deceased loved one used to handle certain tasks and fill certain responsibilities, and grief makes it difficult to care about the details of daily life.

Talking to others can be challenging, especially for those who are grieving; you may be worried about getting in touch with them or unsure of what to say. Friends and family, on the other hand, can make a person feel loved and supported.

If you have not lost a loved one, you might have unreasonable assumptions of how the grieving person should feel, or how easily they should resume everyday activities and move on with their lives. Create an environment where your friend or family member can feel safe and express their emotions. Allow the bereaved to express and speak about their grief in any way they choose. Concentrate your focus on attentive and compassionate listening. If you are not sure how to help a mourning family member, friend, or co-worker, ask them.

Chapter 20:
Ways to Comfort Someone who has Recently Lost their Mother

T here are meaningful ways to show the person grieving that you support them during this time, whether you send a sympathy card, a loving gift, or provide kind words. Put together a nice bouquet of flowers with cards from the office or take turns in bringing some homemade food to your bereaved co-worker. You would be comforting someone whose life seems to be falling apart.

Although they may not acknowledge your efforts, they are going to read all your cards and embrace the helping hand you gave them when they needed it the most.

Sending a sympathy card is a thoughtful way to show the person grieving that you are mindful of them. It can be hard to brainstorm the right words to put on a sympathy card. Try reminding them that you are there whenever they need you. They can reach out if they require the simplest of things, such as helping with the funeral organization. You may remark how much your relationship with their mother meant to you and make comments about her incredible character. Sending a sympathy card is a gesture that is already enough to show your openness to help. You are free to keep things simple if you are afraid you may say the wrong things.

You may plan a visit to see the bereaved. Make sure you let them know you are coming and ask if your presence is welcome during this difficult time. Planned visits allow you to think about what to say to someone who is grieving the loss of their mother. You can interact on a deeper level because planned trips are more likely to be with close friends or relatives.

You may coincidentally run into the bereaved in public. When you run into someone, assess the scenario first before saying anything. If you notice signals that they do not want to talk, do not take it personally. They may simply not be ready to connect at that time, or they may not feel comfortable doing so in public. If they approach you or show indicators of openness, such as facing you, coming toward you, smiling, or starting to converse, you might inquire about their day or if they require any assistance. For individuals who are grieving, mentioning religious words of comfort can be soothing and compassionate. Ideally, you will appoint someone to get this information and whether the bereaved is religious before bringing up anything of this sort. They may still be angry about their loss and bringing up religion would not be the ideal situation.

If a friend has recently lost their mother, you can certainly express your sympathy. When speaking, keep in mind how close you are. Offering to help them around the house may be a bit too much if that is not the relationship the two of you are used to. Sometimes acknowledging their situation and sending your condolences can be enough.

The mourning process is like an uphill path, and no one person goes through it in the same way. Offering nice, non-judgmental words from your heart is the finest approach for a friend, family member, or acquaintance. Be open to the possibility that your friend's life has radically changed. Grief is not a one-time event; it is a succession of experiences that lasts an entire life. It is okay that your friend will always be different from you. Simply put, give it your all, be present, and expect it to be unpleasant. You are dealing with death after all. You may be surprised at what you learn along the way.

Chapter 21:
What not to say to Someone Grieving

Y ou may have panicked and said things you did not mean to say to someone grieving. This is especially the case if you have never experienced the loss of a parent before and are unable to detect what is appropriate and what is not. Try to avoid saying the following to someone grieving and take note of what would be more acceptable:

1. "How old was she before she died? She lived a long life."

This is never appropriate. Whether their mother died at age forty or ninety-nine, it is never acceptable for a mother to die. Although they may have spent a long, beautiful life together, it can never be enough. One wishes they could cherish their mother's presence forever. So instead of putting a verdict on the life they have lived on earth, simply say you are sorry for their loss and send your condolences.

2. "She is in a better place now."

Unless their mother was terminally ill, and your bereaved friend feels relieved for losing their mother, saying this is never appropriate. This is highly inappropriate if they lost their mother at a relatively young age. This is dependent on one's values. If someone would rather have their mother around even if they cannot do much together, saying this can hurt their feelings.

Others believe more in the pride and dignity of living a life of value rather than the number of years so if dying has released the family members from a burden and alleviated her pain, this may not come across as offensive. Instead, just acknowledge that it may be difficult to choose the right words and let them know you care.

3. "This was meant to be because there is always a reason for everything."

At this point, the bereaved may not comprehend this and will probably never accept it. For them, this is not something meant to happen, and they may struggle with it. Make sure they know they are in your prayers, and you are there if needed.

4. "God desired another angel. It was destined to be."

This can be particularly risky, especially if the bereaved is not religious. As part of grief, they may already feel angry at losing their mother, so affirming that God wanted their mother out of all people can be offensive, to say the least. They can never comprehend how losing their mother is something written somewhere and meant to be. Remember that part of the grieving process is feeling angry and trying to bargain. Saying these things can only exacerbate their emotions during grief. If you do not know what to say, just hug them.

5. "It has been a while since the death, and I was hoping you would be over this by now."

There is no set timeframe for anyone to follow while grieving. They may take more than a year or more. They may be struggling to get through the grief themselves, so reminding them that they are taking too long based on your scale of judgment is the last thing they need. If you notice their bereavement is taking way longer than expected, suggest they seek professional assistance in the form of therapy instead. If they bring up the memory of their deceased mother, you may share the memories you have of her. It means they are comfortable talking about it with you and, in fact, they need to.

6. "I know how you feel. I lost mine a few years ago."

This time around, it is not about you. Avoid comparing their bereavement experience to yours. It has been established well by now that no grief is the same; and although they do not intend to be self-centered, they only need words of comfort. They are not insensitive to the experience you had, but they are struggling now. Just tell them you understand how they feel, and you are there to help.

7. "Pluck up the courage and be strong."

If someone you know has just lost their mother, they can take more than six months to pluck up some courage and go on with their daily lives. So, saying this can come as inappropriate at times while putting pressure on them to not mourn. You may say nothing and just make yourself available whenever they need. Show you are concerned and ask if you can help in any way. Make sure they know you are available. On the anniversaries of the deceased's death, marriage, and birthday, it may be helpful to check in with the bereaved, as these can be particularly tough events.

8. "Time will heal."

If you have experienced a mother's yourself, you know very well that time can never heal such a loss. It can get better because the bereaved learns to live with the loss and the void left behind; but there is never a time when they can get over it. Instead, tell them you understand that this is difficult, and you are there to listen if they ever want to talk.

9. "Try and focus on the good memories you had."

If someone you know has recently lost their mother, one of their major worries is exactly they had so many memories and are unable to experience them anymore. This can be something nice to say to someone who has lost their mother - but not immediately after the loss. You may remind them of this later when they have started to move on through the grief process. If you notice they are struggling, you may remind them to look at it from a different perspective. Remind them to celebrate their mother's life; and although they are unable to make memories with her again, they can look back at the beautiful moments they enjoyed.

10. "You have a lot to be grateful for."

Right after the loss, this comment must be avoided. Now they are feeling like the whole world is falling apart and are alone to handle it. They are going through a tragic event and the least thing they are right now is grateful. Grieving is not about being selfish, and it happens naturally without allowing one to exert control over the process. Even if someone who has lost their mother has much to be grateful for, they cannot see it at the moment.

Try asking your friend or family member who is grieving, how they are feeling. Grief can greatly alter moods and feelings and asking them how their mood is on a particular day means you care and want them to update you on the progress they are making, if any. You can make it clear that you are available to talk. Whether it is a colleague or friend, tell them you are going to be in the staff canteen if they want to talk.

Reassure them that you are going to be there for X amount of time and will remain there whether they decide to come and talk or not. This alleviates the pressure but gives them the freedom and comfort to come if they want to. If you are at a loss for words while a friend is pouring their heart out, it is fine to tell them that no words can change how they are feeling, and there is nothing you can say to make the situation any better. Make sure they know you are available to help them get through it. Sometimes just being present is all they need.

Offering practical may also be the one thing they need. You can offer to buy groceries or walk the dog. They may refuse a couple of times but may accept occasionally. It is important to offer help constantly. With their fluctuating emotions, they may refuse help one day but feel like they need it on another day. Remember that grief never goes away, and they may need your help months after the loss.

If you go a walk in the park, ask if they want to come along. It may be that the first and second time you meet, there is complete silence between you two. There may come times where they feel comfortable enough to speak up. If you had stopped offering help after the first time it was refused, they may have not found the courage to speak now. Normalize their reaction to grief and make sure they know they are not off base. Ask them to talk about their mother and the memories you shared.

Recalling memories can light joy in their heart because they are reminiscing the good times spent together.

Chapter 22:
Moving Forward is not Moving on

L osing a loved one is an emotionally charged and painful experience. Coping with loss, on the other hand, can be a profoundly personal experience. It might sound petty, but grief allows you to appreciate the beauty of daily things like sunsets, seasonal changes, and a child's success with a newfound strength. You know the importance of friends and family and how insignificant material objects are unless they assist you in achieving happiness.

It is easy to make progress in your life with a little work. You may go through multiple stages of grieving on the way to feeling better, but these phases are not common to all. Trying to forget or avoid the suffering only makes it harder long term.

It is important to face and consciously cope with your loss in order to recover. You are supposed to dust yourself off, throw on a new sweater, and get back to normal as quickly as possible in today's culture. People used to completely surrender to their sorrow centuries before, even going so far as to wear black mourning clothes for months at a time.

The all-black apparel regimen was designed to grant bereaved survivors some much-needed cultural freedom. You do not have to wear a symbolic black veil, but you should be honest about the need for time to recover. People will value your needs better if you are frank about your sorrow. You may still wear black clothes in your culture, lasting from a few days to weeks.

Switching to normal clothing or going back to wearing a uniform at work does not mean you have moved on; and no, you are not being disrespectful to your late mother. Starting to isolate yourself for some time and then starting to socialize in small groups occasionally, does not mean you have forgotten that you recently lost someone so precious.

This can be difficult to believe at the time, but after huge life setbacks, everyone keeps moving forward every day. You should do it, too. Time will lessen the intensity of the unexpected, the searing pain of loss, as well as your emotions; but feelings of loneliness and disappointment will never go away entirely.

Accepting and welcoming your new normal should assist in making peace with your experiences. There is no best way to feel when faced with a mountain of sorrow. Maybe you are a sobbing wreck, or maybe you are a joke-telling robot. Regardless of what some say, anywhere you land on the scale is perfect.

Allow no one to tell you how you should feel, and do not tell yourself either. No one else can tell you that it is time to move on or get over your grief; it is yours. Allow yourself to feel whatever you want, without fear of being judged. You can never move on after grieving the death of your mother.

A mother's passing leaves a huge absence in your life. Initially, while grieving, you experience emptiness, and it seems like you may never enjoy the days to come. Over time as you grieve, you learn to deal with the loss. You learn to grief while memorializing your mother. You learn to live with the void and remember the good times you spent.

The grief in your life remains however, where before it took over your life, hindering the minimal daily activities. Over time, you learn to live with it and adjust around the void left behind by the loss of your mother.

Once you end the grieving and have reached the acceptance stage, you can stand looking at that photograph of your mother and you on the bedside table. You allow yourself to talk to your mom's friends if you see them in public.

A particular song on the radio may bring you many nice memories of your mother rather than sorrow. People may encourage you to move on because grief is often associated with fear. You fear that you will never adjust to a new life without your mother, and you may never share beautiful experiences without her around.

Some even suggest putting this experience behind and letting go. This can come across as if her life did not matter to you and that the connection you had has an expiration date. It also implies that she can be replaced. If you are grieving such a loss right now, you know this is not the case. It is understandable to feel like you want to tick off grief and strike it off your to-do list - as if it was a chore because grief is not a pleasant thing to go through, and it is sad.

It should be accepted to grieve; and once the death has been accepted, you can go on with your daily activities. You may still have bad days, which is to be excepted.

Grieving for your mother years after the loss may give you comfort because after so many years pass, you are still able to look at a photograph of the two of you and reminisce about her presence. You do not have to get over grief; in fact, you never will. You do not have to look for the same life you had when your mom was still around because you will never find it. Life is going to be different now, and you can learn to adjust to this new life, without forgetting the beautiful memories you shared.

Chapter 23:
Strategies to Finding Happiness Again

S taying in the roughness of loss without moving on to a lighter state is a deeply unsettling way of living. Indeed, life may never be the same after the death of a loved one like your mother. However, if you want it to be, recovery and learning to live again are possible and, in most cases, inevitable. While the loss will still be felt, the pain need not be as serious.

It is perfectly natural to be depressed after a significant loss. What happens after the grieving process is completed determines whether an individual can be happy again. It has a lot to do with the desire to step forward. Many people refer to it as a hole. However, the pain will not be as sharp and intense as it was at first.

It is normal to be sad after a death. What happens after you have been through the mourning process and how you continue to live - the moving forward aspect - is entirely dependent on how you work through grief and continue with your new normal.

Working through the grieving process and enabling it to run its course is necessary before an individual can fully understand that they can be happy again. It can take a long time for certain people to reach the stage of mourning that includes hope and the desire to be happy again. The bereaved person must realize on a deep level that it is possible to feel happy without dishonoring the deceased. When an individual has experienced a significant loss, finding the drive and motivation to seek happiness can be extremely difficult. Here is how:

Take baby steps. Allow the mourning process to run its course. Do not be in a hurry. You cannot be completely content again until the strength of your sorrow subsides. Work through all your feelings and emotions, including remorse, extreme pain, extreme sadness, intense rage, and everything else.

Focus on what is important. People should concentrate on themselves and what they can do to regain their happiness, as well as their spending time and energy living and caring for their families and loved ones. When something joyful happens in your life, acknowledge it and choose IT over the negative aspects of grief.

Give happiness a new meaning. When you cannot fill the hole in some way, you need to try something different to relieve the pain. Try to discover new things or experiences that will bring you joy. Learning to live again may entail an adjustment in attitude and thinking, whether it is the personal satisfaction of achieving goals, spending more time with family, or taking up a new hobby. Keep in mind that adjusting to life after a loss is not a simple task. Things can never be the same again, but it is possible to be happy while being different.

Keep a journal. Reserve five minutes at the end of the day to write one to five things that made you happy. Even if they happened but you did not acknowledge them as being joyful or refused to let them make you happy, write them down. Identifying such moments can make it easier to identify these moments and help you accept them in the future. This can practically make you feel blessed and aware that positive things are still happening despite the grief you have felt or are still feeling.

Capture joyful moments in photographs. Take photos of the small things that make you happy. If you enjoyed watching the sunshine this morning, grab your phone and take a photo of it. Eventually, you can have an album full of positivity as a constant reminder of the things that make you happy.

Make a list of things you enjoyed doing before the loss. List the things you enjoyed doing with your mom before she died. This can include weekend getaways, having coffee at your favorite cafe, or watching movies together. You may not start doing these things after the loss until years after grieving, and that is acceptable. Listing these things will help you identify what triggers your sadness, if done very close to the loss, but can help you know what you need to start incorporating back in your life slowly when you feel ready.

Celebrate life. While the grief of your loss is genuine and must be felt, the time will come to resume your own life. You will come to recognize the loss of a loved one as a fact if you work through the grief. Without your mother by your side, you will be able to enjoy your life. You are in charge of your grieving and bereavement. Above all, be kind to yourself and remember that one day you could wake up with less pain and life will go on.

It is not your fault that unfortunate events occur. It is natural to point the finger at yourself because there is nothing you might have done differently to change the outcome. Life is a blessing. It is impossible to predict when or how it will finish for anyone. It is important to be true to oneself and those who love you.

Respect yourself, enjoy the simple moments, forgive yourself for past mistakes, and love those around you as if it were your last day. It can be difficult to believe that you will ever be happy again. When life-altering events occur, those experiencing them sometimes feel as though life is over. Although a mourning phase is almost certainly inevitable, there might be a ray of hope at the end of the tunnel. It is possible to regain your happiness. Though life will almost certainly never be the same, healing and relearning to live are both possible.

Chapter 24:

Becoming a Parent after Losing Your Mother

Y ou may find your mind wandering from your present-moment elation to think, "I wish she was here", while celebrating graduations, promotions, new homes, weddings, marriages, births, grandbabies, and big and small wins. The idea of becoming a parent after the death of a parent tends to throw a tumult of bittersweet thoughts and feelings for grieving people. Parent-child relationships and family dynamics are so diverse that what works for one person cannot work for another.

If your parent died before your child was born, you may feel bereft and sad because you never got to tell your Mom the good news. Others daydream about how they might have announced their pregnancy in a more personal or elaborate way. And while most people imagine newly expecting parents to be bursting with joy the moment they learn they are having a kid; the reality is that the prospect of becoming a parent evokes a wide range of emotions, from joy and apprehension to fear. You would have loved to introduce them to their grandmother.

When you consider how much they would have loved each other, it seems sad that their paths will never cross. It is difficult to watch your friend's parents attend soccer games and school events, realizing that this is something your parent never got to do. Your child can never have Grandma to encourage them in life. If you are about to give birth to your first child, you wish you could grab the phone and call them to ask her for advice.

You wish you could have your mother watch your kids while you run errands. Most importantly, you wish you could share the joys of raising your kids with her. You would love for her to be there when they utter their first words or take their first baby steps. You wish you could eventually teach them to call her Grandma. Even if you have other people to help and encourage you, no one can fill the gap left by your mother because it is always that one parent's support and guidance that you crave.

It is hard seeing your child grow without a grandparent because in their childhood, you could see yours. Seeing childhood through the eyes of an adult can help you interact with your parents' memories in new ways, feel grateful for all they gave you, and focus on familiar and cozy memories.

Although it is hard to raise a kid on your own, doing it without your mother by your side can be harder. Your child should provide you with a new sense of joy and purpose in life. Becoming a mother or a father while still grieving the loss of your parent can help you see the light. Her death can be a distraction while you focus all your time and energy on raising a child.

You will be passing on your values and beliefs to your child, after having them passed on from your parents to you. Although not around physically, they can still live on. You can continue the bond you had with your mother with your own child.

Once they grow to a certain age, you may start sharing memories with them. The rituals you implement with your family are the ones brought to you by your parents; hence you are carrying the legacy. If you struggled to understand some decisions your mother had made when she was still alive and raising you, you may be able to understand them now that you are going through the same experience.

Having a child after losing your mother is not the solution to overcoming grief. However, if you are moving forward with your life and have become pregnant, you may sadly miss her presence. Just know that this new chapter in life is going to bring you closer to your deceased mother.

Chapter 25:
Ways to Heal After the Loss

If you experience a loss because of aging, a long battle with cancer, an accident, sudden illness, traumatic incident, or suicide, it can interrupt your life or leave you feeling numb or hopeless. Below are ideas that could be useful in helping you heal:

Explore mindfulness and meditation.

Mindfulness is the recognition and non-judgmental perception of the present moment. The mind's natural inclination is to categorize our experiences as positive or negative, good or bad, and then try to stop or numb out the unpleasant ones, such as grief. You cannot numb your suffering selectively without also numbing positive feelings like joy. Enable yourself to experience the pain of grief and simply accept it with compassion. When you can open your heart to pain, you can start to thaw the emotional numbness, allowing you to be open to more joy.

Practice self-care. Eat well, get enough sleep, and keep your body active and fit. Get out into nature, breathe some fresh air, and let your senses take in the wonder of the natural world. Consider developing a gentle yoga practice. Instead of constantly doing, set aside time to just be.

Turn to writing as an outlet. Writing is a type of therapy. Try outlining what happened and how you feel about it. If it feels right, do the exercise four times a week. If it feels overwhelming, pause and do something else that is calming, such as drinking a cup of warm tea, taking a warm bath, going for a walk, or listening to soothing music, then come back to the writing later if you feel up to it. Although this may seem like trigger for sadness short-term, it has been proven to be beneficial in the long run.

Chose creativity. Painting, drawing, taking photos, creating collages, knitting, or other arts and crafts that express your feelings can be used in addition to writing about your loss if you cannot find words to convey your feelings.

Enjoy the little moments. Take time to enjoy something pleasurable with your senses, such as admiring a beautiful flower and inhaling its scent, seeing the bright blue sky, listening to music, or experiencing something wondrous in nature. If you are having trouble finding enjoyment in basic events, try something easy like loving the sensation of cold water, enjoying the smell of soil after the rain, or feeling the sand beneath your feet. Take a few minutes to savor the moment and pay attention to how your body, heart, and mind feel. Then think about it many times during the day.

Give your loss a meaning. Identify ways in which the loss has helped you evolve or become more resilient to stress to find value in it. When you have gotten through the worst of your grief and are well on the way to recovery, think about how to use your loss experience to help others, the community, or the world in general.

Allow feelings of joy. It is just as necessary to practice opening oneself to joy as it is to be present with sorrow. Make room for the things you enjoy and allow yourself to feel happy again. Remember that feeling happy is not disrespectful. Your mother would have not wanted you to feel anything less than happy if she were still around.

Have a good time. Loss serves as a reminder that life is invigorating. Use the time of loss to reflect on your own life and begin to ask whether you are living a life full of joy, doing what you love, and experiencing meaning.

Begin to live deliberately, choosing how you want to your life. Consider this an opportunity to make incremental improvements that could help you live more mindfully.

Loss is unavoidable in life, but it does not have to be a source of hopelessness. You can grow a sense of internal refuge that prepares you to face whatever life throws your way if you take the time to develop your spiritual journey, cultivate the heart, and be present for whatever occurs. You must find aspiration as you learn to reconcile being present with your sorrow with opening yourself to joy. You might also discover that by opening your heart to your sorrow and joy, you gain a greater sense of aliveness than you had before the loss!

Chapter 26:
Seeking Help

When they lose someone as precious as their mother, most people feel a deep sadness. There are some things you can do if these emotions start impacting your life. If you are having trouble coping with stress, anxiety, or depression, help is available. Do not attempt to complete all tasks at once. Do not get caught up in the stuff you cannot alter.

Try not to convince yourself that you are lonely. To cope with loss, avoid using alcohol, smoking, gambling, or medications, as these all lead to poor mental health. Although grief is a normal process, it does not come easy to anyone. Even if you go through grief in the traditional way, you may still require assistance. If your grief turns into the complicated kind, you may highly benefit from assistance.

See your doctor if you are struggling to cope with stress and anxiety. If you are stuck in a low mood for a long time after the death, seek counseling. The best advice is to confide in and speak to someone who understands and empathizes with you - someone who can really assist with your grief. It could be a friend, neighbor, family member, doctor, or therapist. If you are advantageous enough to have a sympathetic friend or family member, you do not need licensed grief therapy. You may have friends with similar experiences and know they are there to listen. Confide in them and see if talking helps your depression.

Most hospitals, medical centers, physicians, and funeral directors can connect you with a grief counseling program in your area. Alternatively, look in the local phone book or on the internet. There are excellent online grief support programs that are both convenient and completely private.

Do not get discouraged if it does not yield positive results right away. It is possible that you have not found the right person for you. Do not hesitate to ask for a different therapist or do your own research. There must be a connection between you and the therapist for the therapy to work.

Community meetings can be beneficial at times. However, if you do not find them useful, move on. Some are excellent, although others might not be. The dynamics of the group are important. Some work while others do not. It can be difficult to listen to other people who are sad. Counselors, too, must consult a specialist from time to time because they are exposed to so much tragedy. It is more difficult when you are fragile. While it can be comforting to know you are not alone, these groups should be approached with caution. Move on if you feel it is making things harder because you are carrying too much of other people's sorrow. Find a cheerful, strong friend with whom you can share enjoyable activities.

The internet is no exception. There are several bereavement sites available these days, including those dedicated to specific forms of loss. These can be extremely helpful but use caution. Do not waste your time hearing about other people's tragedies. You may find it too draining and depressing. Take solace in the fact that you are not alone in your sorrow and then get on with your life.

Accept that many people feel uncomfortable while attempting to console a grieving person. For many people, grief is a perplexing and often terrifying emotion, particularly if they have not experienced a similar loss. They may be unsure of how to console you and might say or do the wrong things as a result. However, do not let this become an excuse to withdraw into your shell and avoid social interaction. If a friend reaches out to you, it means they care. Lean on your friends and family for support. Even though you take pride in your independence and self-sufficiency, now is the time to rely on the people who care. Rather than ignoring them, draw close to friends and family, spend time with them face to face, and embrace the help offered.

People always want to help but are unsure how, so tell them what you require - whether a shoulder to cry on, assistance with funeral plans, or simply someone to hang out with. Making new friends is never too late even if you do not feel you have someone with whom you can regularly talk with in person.

If you observe a particular religious tradition, you may find comfort in its mourning rites. Spiritual practices that you find important, such as praying, meditating, or attending church should provide comfort. Speak to a clergy member or someone in your religious group if you are having doubts about your religion in the wake of the loss. Speak with a psychiatrist or a bereavement counselor. Find a mental health professional who has experience in grief therapy if the grief becomes too much to handle.

A skilled therapist can assist you in working through intense feelings and overcoming mourning obstacles. Grief is a common human experience for which no special medical care is indicated. Healthcare professionals argue that symptoms of depression can precede grief but may be differentiated from those of grief. Therefore, they suggest that medical therapies such as antidepressant medication could be beneficial. This can be determined by your family doctor or psychiatrist.

Although grief and loss are personal experiences, you do not have to do it alone. Seek help if you feel the need, or coping is not as you had perceived it. If your friends or family members demand you seek professional help, do not refuse. They know you well enough to care about your wellbeing.

Conclusion

Your mother is your first playmate and buddy. She was the one who rocked you when you were a newborn, stitched you up when you were a clumsy youngster, and comforted you as a teen. She advised you on the ins and outs of being a first-time parent and assisted you in planning your wedding. In some ways, your mother was the most important person in your life. The discomfort of her death is incapacitating. You could be fine one minute and then be lying on your bedroom floor in excruciating pain the next. You are probably sitting there nodding your head in agreement if you have lost your mother and you made it this far through the book.

Regardless of what I have written, nothing that can take the pain away, but like everything in life, you can learn to cope with the different stages. The loss of a mother may be the first grief that you sobbed without her by your side. You never get over it. The sorrow can fade, and the profound mourning moments can become fewer, but how can you ever get over losing your mother?

Loss influences every aspect of life and often bring us to a halt. Death serves as a stark reminder that life is fragile and that something bad can happen at any time. No matter how much effort you dedicate, you are not able to truly brace for it. To get to the other side of loss, you must walk a journey of fire and suffering, intense sorrow, and debilitating fear to the position where you can experience the goodness of life and gain a renewed love for your time here.

Understanding this experience and pausing to reflect on what it means to live and die in this universe allow us to emerge on the other side more comfortably, having been turned into a human of deep sensitivity and empathy, not only for the world at large but also for yourself. You will never be able to recover from the loss of someone you care so much for, but you can learn to deal with it.

You can find new ways to communicate with your deceased loved ones, free yourself from fear, and re-open yourself to the world. You have but one chance to grieve over those you love. Do not drive it away or keep yourself occupied the whole time. You may lose the sense of being linked to that person. It is also okay if you feel like your whole world has come crashing down around you! It undoubtedly has.

It is now up to you to work out how to reassemble yourself. Be creative and get a new lease on life. Someone precious about has been taken from you, and your heart has been broken. Anger, sorrow, guilt, fear, and peace are all manifestations of grief. It is unpredictable and tiring at times.

From the moment you receive the terrible news to trying to settle and distribute your late mother's assets, it can be a tragic experience. The funeral organization can take a toll on your mental and physical health. Knowing how to handle the changes can help you survive through this awful journey in the hope of finding light at the end of the tunnel.

Know when and how to ask for help if you feel that some of your symptoms or feelings are alarming. If someone close to you, indifferent to their gender, has lost their mother, you now know what questions to ask and how they might be dealing with the loss. There is going to be a new life with a new norm as you start facing the loss. You may come across your late mom's presence everywhere you look, especially right after the loss.

There are ways to deal with this, so embrace them or avoid them as you please. If you feel you are struggling in your community or at work because of the loss, now you know why and how to overcome it. If you have committed mistakes or feel like you are going to be filled with regret after losing your mother, you know you can deal with and overcome it.

To recapitulate, there are techniques and ways to overcome grief without disrespecting your mother. You may be faced with other challenges as if your mother's death is not enough already. You may be an expectant mother or father who recently lost their mother and feel like there is too much to deal with right now. Know that your child is a blessing, and your mother would have not wanted it any other way.

There are ways this new milestone in life can help you move forward from your mother's death. While staying in touch with your mother's memory, you can pass on the values your mother gave you to your child. You may relive your childhood while your child is growing up to help memorialize your mother and celebrate her years on earth. If someone close to you has lost their mother, by now you know what to say and what to avoid. You know how to be a support system and help them get through this tragic event.

Allow no one to tell you that what you are experiencing is exaggerated and never allow someone to push you to move on. Acknowledge the loss and know you will never forget your mother's memory. Learn to live and grow around your grief. You can succeed while always remembering your mother and the lovely memories you shared.

Death puts everything in perspective and may have you becoming careless about things that once mattered to you. The little things you used to enjoy like hobbies now seem trivial. You may feel as if you can never go back to enjoying reading or taking a walk in the park. This is perfectly normal, especially close to the death of your mother. But learning to incorporate a daily self-care routine should help you cope.

Take the book's tips for incorporating meditation and finding an outlet for your emotions. Try journaling, take short trips, and get out there and socialize. Learn how getting back to work at your own pace will help you move forward. Learn to accept the help offered by your friends and allow yourself to delegate tasks if you are not able to complete them right now.

Grief is a highly personal experience, with a different feeling every day. You may require many weeks, or you may grieve for years. A mental health specialist is a valuable guide for vetting thoughts and seeking a sense of assurance about these very strong and weighty emotions.

You will eventually find reasons to smile again following your mother's passing. This is one of the most meaningful ways you can commemorate your mother and the love you have for her. Regain your joy. Laugh out loud. Love with all your heart. Live your life as though it were your mother's. Do not fight your feelings when you miss your mother. Permit yourself to miss her.

There is no proper way to grieve, and the process does not have to last a certain amount of time. Over time, the discomfort becomes more bearable. Nobody can take your mother's place. There can never be another mother in this world. On so many levels, she is irreplaceable. Taking care of your mental well-being and keeping friendly relations with family and friends will help you overcome this turmoil.

Getting on with your life is not disrespectful. You now know better than to let yourself drown in regret and sorrow. Your mother would not have wanted you to do that. You can carry on with living while carrying your mother's values and legacy with you. Your mother's death is not an excuse to let go of life; it is another reason to keep striving.

Let these words fuel your dedication and enthusiasm to succeed in life, in relationships, at work, and being a parent yourself. It is not final goodbye. Go and make your mother proud of who you become because of her!

Author's Note

Dear reader,

I hope you enjoyed my book. Please don't forget to toss up a quick review on Amazon, I will personally read it! Positive or negative, I'm grateful for all feedback.

Reviews are so helpful for self-published authors and your feedback can make such a difference for my book!

Thanks very much for your time, and I look forward to hearing from you soon.

Sincerely,

Melanie